Get off the Bus

Depression, Anxiety & Obsession

Steven A. Szykula, Ph.D.

"Dr. Steve"

GET OFF THE BUS: DEPRESSION, ANXIETY & OBSESSION

Steven A. Szykula, Ph.D.

First Printing: 2014

Notice of Rights

Printed and bound in the United States of America.

Cover Design: Devan Bailey

Edited by: Walter Mason

To my clients, colleagues, friends and family, thank you very much for showing me the way. It has been an honor for me to join so many in support of their quest to get off the bus and improve their lives.

Namaste and thank you to Hope Allred for inspiring me to start the book and to Rocky Anderson for his wisdom to finish it.

Steven A Szykula, Ph.D.

Dr. Szykula's work has spanned across three decades during which time he has provided psychological counseling and evaluation services to thousands of adults and children. Dr. Szykula has contributed to numerous articles and books on psychotherapy, counseling and parenting. His sense of humor and wisdom make him a sought after speaker. His books and presentations enable others to apply new practical knowledge and skills to reduce problems and achieve a more meaningful life.

To reach people he cannot counsel face-to-face, Dr. Steve writes practical "self-help" books, books on parenting and books used by counselors and therapists. Raised in Connecticut, he now lives and works in Salt Lake City, Utah. His multi-disciplinary clinic, Comprehensive Psychological Services, serves thousands of clients every year and is considered to be one of the best clinical practices for psychological counseling and therapy in the West. Further information about Dr. Steve, his books and presentations and Comprehensive Psychological Services can be found on his website: www.wecanhelpout.com.

Exchanges between clients and their therapist are included throughout this book. Personal details, situations, names, occupations, and symptoms have been altered to protect privacy.

The principals that are emphasized in this book may be integrated into anyone's life. Readers who are participating in medication therapies or various talk therapies should continue with these if progress is being made. The stories, therapy case examples and principals discussed in this book are universal, enhance and do not compete with other forms of treatment.

Contents

Chapter 1

Riding the Bus

How much of your day is spent worrying? Do you spend time endlessly resenting and regretting the past? Do you procrastinate? These are common problems my clients have experienced. In my work, I refer to these patterns of thinking and emotion as *riding the bus*—with the implied goal of *getting off the bus* and into life.

Riding the bus can affect one's life in serious and intense ways. Do depressing or anxious feelings and thoughts prevent you from living your life to its fullest? Does trauma from your past make poor decisions in the future seem inevitable? Do you put yourself down or "stress out" about what others may think of you?

Some of these questions reflect patterns associated with conditions like depression, anxiety, and post-traumatic stress disorder. Indeed, you may suffer from a current state of mind that will not shut down as it cycles through thoughts, delivering compulsive urges to use drugs, alcohol, or the Internet. Or you may suffer from anxiety and panic that make you so self-conscious that you fail to reach your goals.

Being stuck riding the bus can rob you of your life. I wrote this book to help you get off the bus and into healthy engagement with a meaningful and fulfilling life.

Bus rides can disrupt your day, your week—even your life. Allow me to illustrate how dysfunctional thoughts and feelings associated with procrastination, wishful thinking, self-doubt and worry play havoc with your mood and your thinking in the stories below. As you read below, think about the bus rides that rob you of precious moments and richness in your own life.

Procrastination: The Kitchen Floor

"Procrastination is the thief of time."

— Charles Dickens, *David Copperfield*

The kitchen floor weighed heavily on my mind. It was ripe for cleaning. The floor and I glared at each other for about thirty minutes. Slowly, procrastination caused me to feel heavy, lethargic, and depressed. I felt energy leaving my body. Here I was, the first day of the weekend, and I was sinking into a gloomy mood. Stalling, I made another pot of coffee. I begrudgingly thought about the tools and cleaners I would need to clean the kitchen floor. I wondered where I had stored them all. I started to resent having to clean the floor on my weekend. How long would it take to clean the kitchen floor? Would I find the cleaning supplies? With these questions, my mood sank even lower.

Still in my pajamas, I moved very slowly. I looked at the clock and noticed I had been thinking off-and-on about cleaning the kitchen floor for nearly two hours now. My mood plummeted to an even lower level, gradually cascading to depression and no energy. I glared at the clock; almost all of Saturday morning had passed. In a flurry of motivation, I cranked up the stereo with the best Motown selection I could find. I located the cleaning supplies, got down on my hands and knees and began scrubbing the kitchen floor. Twenty minutes later, with a smile across my face, the floor was clean.

Who has not experienced something like this—being held hostage by thoughts about a task when the task itself only requires a little focused effort? Let's consider the pattern that underlies this behavior. In this example of procrastination, we observe that over-thinking about cleaning the kitchen floor results in a lethargic and depressed mood. In this case, dwelling on such unproductive thoughts and their attendant emotions exemplify what riding the bus means. We observe that when the bus rider is fed up with the ride, he focuses and engages in the task, cleaning the floor. When engaged in cleaning the floor the negative thoughts and emotions dissipate. The task is completed and our example procrastinator gets back to experiencing a more productive and satisfying life.

For many people, procrastination is a way of life that results in distress and diminished satisfaction. Yet the addictive power of riding the bus—that is, dwelling on thoughts and emotions—can be difficult to stop. Awareness of the thought patterns underlying procrastination is essential to being able to reduce or stop these behaviors. Rather than allowing this pattern to occur and recur, robbing hours at a time, my goal is to help readers identify these patterns promptly, if not to avoid bus rides altogether, to make the rides as brief as possible.

In another example of procrastination and overthinking, a working mother procrastinates and then dwells on her lack of results. This cycle causes her stress, while robbing her of the opportunity to fully enjoy time with her family.

Don't Bring Your Work Home: The Dreaded Weekly Report

"Never leave till tomorrow that which you can do today."

— Benjamin Franklin

At the end of every week, I am required to submit a report to the corporate office. This report reflects the work I have completed during the week. It also keeps the corporate office updated as to what is happening in the field. Each week, I dread preparing this report. I often resent that the corporate office wants me to spend fifty hours doing my job and then work two additional hours writing them how I did it. Corporate expects the report at the end of the day on Friday. However, I know they aren't going to look at it until Monday morning. Consequently, I habitually procrastinate writing it, finding myself preparing the report at the last minute every Sunday night. The report has to be submitted via the Internet before the system goes down at 9:30 PM.

At the end of the day on Friday, finally happy to be done with my workweek, I slap my laptop shut and turn my attention to the weekend. Almost immediately, I start to worry: first that I won't remember my activities of the workweek, then that I need to report on Sunday night. I immediately rationalize that I deserve a break now and that I can do the report later. I decide to be done with work for a few days.

On Saturday night just before going to sleep, I find myself dreading the weekly report again. The thought just keeps resurfacing. Then again on Sunday morning as I awaken, rubbing my tired eyes, lying in bed, I think, "Ugh — I have to get that weekly report done today." "But not yet, I will go get some coffee, maybe read the newspaper, and try not to think about work." I go about the activities of the day with the thought of the report repeatedly nagging at me. I wonder why the muscles in my neck are so tense and I find it difficult to focus and enjoy the time with my kids.

As the afternoon presses on, I start to feel sick to my stomach. I want to lie down and take a nap. I go through my day with my kids and I am only half conscious, just going through the motions. Sighing, I think about the unfinished weekly report off and on throughout the day. Then at around 6:00 PM, my 8-year-old son runs into the living room and announces, "I have a school project due tomorrow!" I pull out his backpack and realize it's going to take us a couple of hours to get this project done. Adding to my stress is the fact that we are going to have to go to the store and get some supplies in order to complete it. I think to myself, "Why on earth didn't he tell me about this sooner? He's known about the project for a whole week." I have no idea how we are going to get his project done before he needs to go to bed. I begin to panic because I must also get my weekly report completed before the server goes down at 9:30 PM. My mind races and my blood pressure rises.

By the skin of our teeth, we complete the school project. I help my son get ready for bed. I look at the clock and panic. There is no possible way for me to complete the weekly report tonight. I realize I will have to get up at 5:00 AM to submit the report before corporate opens at 8:00 AM on the East Coast. I try to sleep, but I toss and turn stressing over the weekly report. I worry that I will sleep through the alarm. My stomach is in a knot.

I awaken at 4:00 AM and my mind continues to race with anxiety. I decide to get up and orient myself. At about 5:00 AM I compile my notes and write up a report that summarizes the events of my last workweek. I electronically submit the report. I vow to get the report completed and submitted before 6:00 PM next Friday from now on. I think, "Why do I ever put this report off? I should always do it on Friday so I can enjoy my weekend."

Repetitive thinking, wishing, and worrying can derail you from progressing in life. In the next account you will see that thoughts alone can become tremendous obstacles to accomplishing goals. Wishful thinking—as opposed to accepting reality and moving forward—is often a repetitive pattern of thought that hinders healthy activity and increases distress.

Interview Anxiety: The Graduate

"Anxiety does not empty tomorrow of its sorrows,

but only empties today of its strength."

— Charles Spurgeon

I graduated from college assuming that my college degree would guarantee me a good job. I was wrong. There are no guarantees. I worked at a golf course through school and could not find a better job after graduation. I thought after working there for eight years and passing golf credential tests, I should at least be earning more than minimum wage without benefits. I was recently passed over for a promotion in favor of someone who was older. I also thought that he might have interviewed better than me. I was very nervous during my interview. I dwelled on the fact that I became terribly nervous before job interviews.

I told myself over and over again how unfair interviews were, how I sucked at interviews, and how I would never get a job that required an interview. I wished that I could get a job without getting interviewed. I considered myself a loser. I worried about what others might think of me. I wished I were different—and I made myself sick with these thoughts.

Deep down I knew these thoughts were not actually true. Yet I could not stop thinking this way. It made me sick with depression and anxiety. My thoughts had me convinced I would never succeed in finding a job. They froze me. I completed a few online applications. My girlfriend's mother helped me scout jobs online but this only seemed to add pressure! I felt like I was such a disappointment to her now.

My obsessive thinking and worrying sidetracked me from studying for my second level golf-pro test and from my online job search. People gave me advice to go to employers in-person and to ask to meet with the hiring manager. I froze up even more. I thought over and over again, "I don't do that," "That's not me," "That would be rude," and "I would be bothering potential employers." I was anxious about going out and walking into a situation cold. I thought to myself, "What if I stumbled on my words? After all, I suck at interviews."

I noticed that bad days were the result of not having a schedule or an activity to focus on, like golf or work. On these days, I was overtaken by my thoughts. I would think about what other people might think of me and how they might be judging me. I would then turn on myself, thinking about how I couldn't succeed, or how I should have taken a different direction in college—and on and on. My self-esteem would plummet and I would feel like crying. Several times, I considered going to a doctor to get medication.

I began to notice that I had good days and bad days. When I had a good day, I woke up with the alarm, engaged in a schedule that included job searches, interviews and resume drops. I also scheduled activities and worked.

The young man in the case scenario above clearly is thinking and dwelling on negative self-judgment and the possible negative judgment of others about him. In his case riding the bus was debilitating. Not only was the thinking excessive, it also drove severe negative emotions like anxiety and depressed mood. These emotions are also a bus, from which one wants to depart quickly in order to get on with life.

The graduate discovered that he got off the bus and enjoyed the feeling of moving forward on days when he was fully engaged in a busy schedule that even included completing job applications and interviews.

The *Kitchen Floor*, *Weekly Report* and *The Graduate* illustrate the effects of riding the bus—engaging in dysfunctional and repetitive thinking and emotion. What are the examples of dysfunctional thinking and emotion in *your* life? Boarding the bus by overthinking, one finds his or her thoughts can lead to depressed feelings, reduced energy, and even physical symptoms. Conversely, intensely focusing and engaging in productive activity leaves behind the cycling of negative thoughts and their attendant emotions. When you ruminate and procrastinate you create unnecessary emotional distress—in other words, you are riding the bus. Getting off the bus first requires that you increase your awareness of the bus and is then followed by focusing and engaging in the task at hand.

Left unchecked, these thoughts and feelings may develop more serious distress, which often culminates in emotional problems. Although entirely eliminating these patterns of thinking and feelings is impossible, interrupting them and refocusing intensely on healthy, productive activities can reduce the number of rides and make getting off the bus much easier.

Chapter 2

The Road to Anxiety, Depression and Hopelessness

"You may believe that you are responsible for what you do, but not for what you think. The truth is that you are responsible for what you think, because it is only at this level that you can exercise choice. What you do comes from what you think."

— Marianne Williamson, *A Return to Love*

Have you ever experienced a major life event that left your thoughts and emotions in a seemingly inescapable cycle of hopelessness? Maybe it was the death of a loved one, loss of a job, or a divorce. These life-changing events can begin cyclical thought processes beyond what would be considered a normal reaction to a stressful situation. Following any major life change, you might become vulnerable to repetitive thoughts and feelings. These thought patterns are insidious and can become addicting. They divert you away from living a healthy life and from processing stressful situations with healthy responses, leaving you more vulnerable to life's many obstacles. These cycling thoughts can, and often do, lead to bouts of mental illness.

What follows are stories about my clients who, over time, created their own severe mental suffering that took them to the breaking point. Their bus rides led them to experience extreme depression, anxiety, anger, and hopelessness. Riding the bus almost always comprises a pattern of habitual emotions or repetitive thinking. Assigning the buses more specific names allows us to identify the kind of thoughts and emotions that are being repeated. In the cases below, my clients were susceptible to multiple bus rides and double-decker bus rides while the active living of their lives slipped away from them.

Depression, Low Self-esteem and Hopelessness

Martha is a young woman who spent most of her days thinking about the critical judgments she thought others, including her parents, had of her. Not an hour went by without her feeling she was behind and guilty for being less accomplished than her peers. She obsessed about what people thought of her. Over and over, she would think that others judged her as a "loser".

Martha isolated herself from friends who were making progress in their personal development and lives. She resented them and presumed to know what they thought of her, much like she presumed to know precisely what her parents thought of her. She ruminated over these assumptions day in, day out. Over time, she convinced herself that her parents and her friends could not care less about her. This pattern of obsessive, assumptive thinking about the imagined negative judgments of others, along with her own self-deprecating judgments, created extreme mood swings, anger, depression, sadness, and hopelessness. Indeed, Martha was riding the bus.

Martha suffered self-deprecating feelings and thoughts on a daily basis. If anyone made a comment that she perceived as negative in any way, Martha would become outraged and vindictive. She would spend hours thinking about what the person said, twisting their motives, interpreting otherwise innocuous comments in a deeply personal way. To say the least, this was exhausting. To escape and buffer the impact of her own thinking and emotional upheaval, Martha became rebellious. She drank heavily and frequently. She partied hard. She sought out and clung to "bad boys," young men who went about their lives irresponsibly and taking risks.

Martha's pattern of dating these players in the party scene enabled her to temporarily distract herself from her own mind and suffering by attaching herself to the *vida loca* that these men brought with them. It was high stimulation, lots of people, lots of laughs and lots of intoxication. Many of the men were bright and college educated but none were trustworthy. Deep down Martha knew this. But they provided her an escape from her suffering mind.

Over and over, it seemed that no matter whom she hung out with, they would eventually "dump" her and at times even strand her miles away from where she lived. Martha's blood would boil.

She wanted to retaliate. Her head spun with anger. She rode the anger bus for months after these episodes. Each of these relationships afforded Martha only temporary relief from her feelings and thoughts of her low self-esteem, her lack of progress in her life and what she thought about how her parents would judge her. In the end, hooking up with these guys only led to further misery and obsessive anger, while leaving Martha's life in continuous turmoil and suffering.

When Martha was not mindlessly partying, she spent almost every waking hour suffering with feelings of guilt, resentment and anger. For moments Martha would temporarily realize that she was smart, personable and capable. These moments would quickly pass as Martha had almost become addicted to her repetitive thoughts of how far behind her peers she was and how it was too late to "catch up."

Martha's thinking patterns kept her stuck. Her internal negativity was endless. Martha suffered and made little progress toward her life goals because she dwelled on her assumptions about what others thought of her. This dynamic was only worsened by her anger toward the men who would eventually treat her badly. This cycle derailed Martha's life.

One night Martha was partying hard. She drank too much. Feeling that she could still safely drive home, she left the party early. She was pulled over for drunk driving. Among her penalties was court-ordered counseling. Martha had never gone to counseling before; she avoided it because she knew how emotional it would be for her. Now her freedom and privilege to drive was in the balance. She had to comply.

To Martha's surprise, she liked her counselor. In counseling Martha felt protected and safe to share her thoughts and feelings. Martha knew she was off track and not making progress toward her life goals and shared this with the counselor.

In counseling Martha learned about the mind and how internally focusing on thoughts and feelings was addicting and seldom led to being productive. She learned to separate her sense of her own identity and power away from the thoughts. She learned to commit her concentration to the present and she learned to commit to what she truly valued: education, interesting people, time with her family and making friends who led a good life.

We can see that Martha's bus rides reflected her negative thinking about herself and her beliefs about how others judged her. This bus ride sank her mood and fostered her anger, depression and low esteem to the point where she quit trying. Her growth and development was frozen as her mind took over. Counseling helped Martha refocus on what she valued and wanted in her life. Counseling helped her raise her awareness of the subterfuge that the bus rides caused. Counseling helped her stay present-focused and follow her plan.

Hopelessness Following Career and Family Losses

Having achieved success as a father and entrepreneur, Phil had once been mentally healthy. Unfortunately, he began to spend most of his time riding the bus. He spent his days dwelling on events that were out of his control, undermining his own mental health. Losing hours at a time, his focus exclusively attended to negative thoughts and feelings evoked by the events over which he lacked any influence.

Phil spent hours alone at his private office, staring at the wall, agonizing over his plight. The district court judge had just ruled on a temporary child custody order based on his ex-wife's false claims that he was an unfit father. His parenting time had been reduced from Thursday through Monday overnights to only Wednesday evening visits. He was outraged and a flood of negative thoughts permeated his mind. Incessant questions of, "Why me?" and, "How could this be happening?" began to dominate his every waking moment. He spent hours each day dwelling on the anger he felt towards the judge. He was exasperated at the injustice and his perceived helplessness. The trial for the final custody decision was six months away.

Phil sat for hours replaying the court proceedings in his head. He worried about the words he spoke in court. He wondered over and over if he should have said anything differently or done something else—something more could have been done, perhaps. "Maybe then the judge would have seen things clearly and I wouldn't be in this mess," he constantly thought to himself.

Phil was naturally a problem solver. However, in this case, incapable of taking matters into his own hands and forging a solution, stuck in his perceived helplessness, he dug deeper and deeper into negative thoughts and anger. As he saw it, there was no way for him to solve this problem. As each week passed, his anger and frustration only grew. At the same time, he neglected the problems in his life that he could address and resolve.

Phil sank deeper into sadness and depression and avoided going home. Instead, he spent more hours alone at his office thinking about the injustice handed down by the court. He overanalyzed the court proceedings as if he could fix the past by thinking about it. If this was not enough, his ex-wife often thwarted his efforts to be a father by encouraging his teenage daughters to make plans with friends during evenings scheduled with him. Each time this happened, Phil was crushed. He became distraught because he would not see his daughters for yet another week. He stewed in his anger towards his ex-wife. On one level, he understood that his daughters loved him, so he felt secure about their love for him. And he knew it was normal for them to want to be involved with their friends and with school. On another level, however, he wondered why they were not defending their time with him, which saddened him.

To make matters worse, Phil's career and financial status were a disaster. Once a successful developer, Phil had over-extended himself by investing his personal fortune into developing luxury homes. The real estate and banking crash resulted in Phil's complete financial demise. Facing bankruptcy and no possibility of sustaining a business as a real estate developer, his mind spun out of control. He was distraught with worry. "Why me?" he wondered, while the thought, "I should have seen this coming," assaulted his thinking again and again. Phil was on many buses that made his life miserable. He was stuck.

Phil experienced bouts of depression. He brooded over many events that had occurred in his life where he had no control. When he wasn't grinding away over his children's custody, he would engross himself in thoughts related to his business failure, his inability to earn money, and his lost career, all of which led to greater emotional turmoil. He assumed people didn't want to be around him now that he was a failure. "Will I ever come out of this?" he wondered.

As Phil pulled away and began to isolate himself, Katie, his new wife, began to panic. A retired schoolteacher, Katie was upbeat and dynamic. Finding and marrying Phil, who she considered her soul mate, made Katie's life complete and meaningful. She begged him to pull himself together, to develop a plan to dig himself out, move forward, and appreciate what they still had and what they could rebuild.

Yet Phil remained frozen. When he looked at Katie, he saw himself as an even greater failure. He now believed he could never make her happy without the money that previously gave them the ability to buy things and do the activities they had enjoyed before his financial demise.

Phil was riding a bus of misery and was addicted to the ride. Most of his time was now spent dwelling on anger, guilt, worry and hopelessness.

Phil exhausted himself with unproductive thoughts and depressed emotions. There was no resolution in sight. Phil's physician prescribed a mood stabilizer, a tranquilizer and sleeping pills. The medications dulled his thoughts, but Phil continued to dwell on the injustice of the system, as well as his professional failure, obsessing, "Why me?" Feeling worthless, he concluded he had no value to anyone. His life spun with despair.

Phil awoke in a hospital bed and learned that he had accidentally overdosed and nearly lost his life. His family thought he attempted to kill himself. Now he was humiliated—another bus ride—because he could not convince them that he did not intend to overdose. These thoughts and feelings of humiliation added to his other constant ruminations. In his perceived helpless state, he gave his wife his medications to dispense to him.

Although he had no intention of killing himself, life at this time did not appeal to Phil. He continued to isolate himself. He dropped deeper and deeper into depression.

Phil entered therapy with me after his release from the hospital. He attended sessions with his wife. In therapy, Phil and his wife, who was very supportive, learned how to get off the bus. Phil learned to focus on what he needed to do to live fully and to develop a new life plan. He learned to focus on spending time with Katie when they would visit his daughter. He learned to focus on what he could do to move forward in a new career. He began to be at peace, focusing on what was in his control to change his situation, rather than riding the bus, which offered no peace or resolution. When he began to dwell on something, he started calling it "the bus," which allowed him to get off of it and refocus on what he valued most. Katie and Phil also began to spend more time together and do things with friends.

Repeatedly focusing on what one's mind delivers can be devastating. Martha, Phil and Sarah became so over-focused and obsessed with anger, resentment, negative self-judgment and hopelessness that they did not want to live. Their work in therapy helped them get off the bus, not by focusing on the bus, but by helping them identify and focus on valued life plans, which helped them focus intensely on the present. One may choose to focus on worry, panic, stress, fear or anger as if they exist in the physical world but one must realize they are only in one's mind.

In the chapters to follow you will learn to identify and avoid the bus—or, when riding the bus, how to get off of it, and stay off as much as possible. You will learn about key elements and skills that will help you experience a more satisfying life that will increase peace of mind and joy. These skills and keys will help you avoid distressing thoughts and feelings allowing you to move forward toward a more fulfilling life.

Chapter 3

Keys to Getting

Off the Bus

Chapters four through seven allow the reader the opportunity to peek into therapy sessions with clients suffering from various symptoms accompanying depression, anxiety and substance abuse. These sessions lend the reader unique insight into methods I offer my clients to face and overcome their problems. I will write of these methods in terms of keys that can get you off the bus and unlock healthy mental activity.

As you read these in-session therapist-client dialogues, take note of pivotal exchanges containing the keys for helping clients (and you, the reader) get off the bus. Remember that these key steps result in the process through which the bus is first identified and then disembarked, which leads to a more peaceful and satisfying life.

The key steps for the process, which are expressed next in detail, include: becoming the observer of your own thoughts and feelings; reducing repetitive thinking; learning present focus; establishing a life plan; seeking out social support and a therapeutic alliance; and, of course, utilizing metaphors to remind you to take back your life by staying off the bus.

After learning about these key steps, look for them to occur in the therapist-client exchanges. Consider how the keys can be applied to your problems, which can lead to a more fulfilling life.

Becoming the Observer

How does it look, feel, and sound to observe your own thoughts? People who consider their thoughts and feelings as observers tend to adjust smoothly to life events, addressing trauma without excessive suffering. A good first step toward healthy mental activity rests in developing the ability to consider your thoughts and feelings as separate from yourself. Becoming the observer of your internal mental processes allows you to identify negative thoughts and feelings as external intruders. This usually results in initial relief, which fosters your ability to problem-solve by freeing your attention from negative emotions and destructive thoughts. In this form of active self-awareness, you *observe* the thought or feeling as opposed to *living* it. Instead of passively accepting these thoughts as part of who you are, you begin to perceive these unproductive thoughts and feelings as bus rides distinctly removed from yourself. The question of whether or not to board each bus is revealed as requiring your consent. From this new perspective, you take back control of your life.

Take a moment right now to try out this practice. Concentrate on the first thought or feeling that pops into your head. Then take notice of the next thought or feeling that pops into your head. Now stand up and lift one foot into the air. Briefly hold this position, balancing on your other foot. Consider your physical constitution: your bones, tendons and muscles. They shift back and forth to maintain your balance. Pay close attention to how the muscles in your foot find stasis. Remain relaxed and breathe. Calmness will promote sensitivity to your body's subtle components; notice muscle twitches, for instance, laboring to keep you stable.

What happened to your thoughts and feelings during the exercise? Where did they go? Are they back now? Are they intruding? Can you experience them metaphorically as buses waiting to be boarded?

Focus on your initial thought or feeling again. Is it you? Or is it something you can observe, apart from you?

I often invite my clients to conduct an illuminating experiment in the comfort and safety of my office. These clients are plagued with repetitive emotional extremes and cyclical thoughts. Among other things, they experience worry, anxiety, and full-blown panic—to the extent, even, that they feel they cannot breathe, let alone work, drive a car, or take care of their children.

I begin, "Now try—I mean *really* try—to make your distress worse. For the next thirty seconds try this."

Please try this now, yourself.

What happened? What did you experience? Could you make your distress worse? Or did your distress get worse when you thought, *Oh no! What if I do make it worse?*

Most people who try this experiment report experiencing the inability to make their distress worse. It only gets worse if their attention shifts from the thought, *I want to increase the distress on purpose*, to the thought, *What if my distress does get worse?*

Many people experience a shifting back and forth. I am sometimes asked, "What if I can make my distress worse?" Then I reply, "That's when you become more than the observer. You become the bus driver, and you control it. If you can purposely drive it to be worse, then you can also purposely drive it to the parking lot and get off the bus."

The vital understanding to derive from this experiment is to subsequently realize that you were looking at distressing thoughts and feelings as separate entities. You, if for a moment, became the observer.

This exercise demonstrates your capacity to begin looking at negative thoughts and feelings as distinct entities undermining your mental health. Far from constituting who you are, they are merely thoughts and feelings. If anything, they obscure who you really are by distancing you from your potential. They are buses—and buses stop and go. As you observe them, you are witnessing them pull up to the bus stop, which we might think of as your awareness. The significance of this, of course, is that you do not have to board. Realize that the more you attend to this new perspective, the more it will develop.

In the therapist-client dialogue in the chapters that follow, you will see how clients learn how to separate themselves from negative thoughts and destructive emotions by becoming the observer.

The question inevitably arises: How can you tell if you are observing and not riding the bus? Many people describe their experience of observation as briefly noticing thoughts and feelings while they slip away, making room for the next thought, or clearing mental space in which to concentrate. To return to the bus metaphor, this is like watching buses pass. This gives you time and space between the bus schedules to engage in life.

Recognizing your dysfunctional thoughts or emotions is to recognize you are on the bus. Identifying these thoughts and emotions before they assume your mental space is to see these buses pulling up. These are both important steps. Getting off the bus is easier if you can conceptualize yourself as an observer of the thoughts running through your mind.

Repetitive Thinking

Why do we have repetitive thoughts and feelings? Because we can. Evolution has blessed us with great abilities to solve problems and avoid danger, which better ensure our survival. Humans have developed so effectively that we do not always have to focus on survival—but at our core, it is our nature.

Given that, if we are often not focused on survival in the external world, we drift inward and create survival-intensity thoughts and feelings. A consequence of this ability is the creation of immense distress, which produces a stress reaction similar to the fight/flight/freeze response you might experience when confronted by the threat of an angry grizzly bear. But there is no bear.

In other words, it's not the growling bear that is chasing us that stimulates our fight/flight/freeze response; it's our own internal thoughts. We think and feel until the threat is gone. In the case of feelings and thoughts however, one must realize that these will always be inside our mind. There is no escaping this. There is only the opportunity to refocus externally.

When we lose focus on living life and we over-focus on thinking and feeling, we often label it depression, anxiety, post-traumatic stress, worry, craving, panic, anger or many other names.

Our highly developed brain's ability to reflect on its own activity is therefore both a blessing and a curse.

However, we can learn to engage our brains in the present. Engaging fully and with as many of our senses as possible is also helpful. To become the observer; to recognize repetitive thinking; to engage in present focus; to engage in valued activities, hobbies and personal interests with a life plan that reflects your values—these are all important components to maintaining a healthy life. However, while intense engagement and present focus are possible, they are a challenge. To face this challenge it takes awareness in conjunction with engagement to move forward in your life.

Have you ever noticed your energy level dropping and your mood suffering on days during which your thoughts about something seem to be stuck on repeat? Did you know that repetitive thinking is a major pattern for people with anxiety and depression? You probably did. But did you know that even repetitive *positive* thinking is associated with depressed moods? In fact, social psychologists studied the effects of daydreaming—a repetitive pattern of positive thought—on college students' moods. Researchers equipped the students with smartphones that prompted the students to log whether or not they were daydreaming at the time of the prompt. At the end of each day, the students self-reported a score of their mood on a rating scale. Results clearly demonstrated that students who daydreamed more than others also more regularly experienced depressed moods.[1]

We are left to conclude that repetitive thinking, positive or negative, is unhealthy. In both cases, it is riding the bus. It does not enhance one's experience of life, nor does it lend itself to an individual's development or survival. The occurrence of repetitive thinking, whether positive fantasies in daydreams or thoughts of impending doom, is monumental. Clearly, the challenge to you in your quest for peace of mind and life satisfaction is to get off the bus, which requires moving away from repetitive, dysfunctional thoughts and emotions.

Recall the skill-development exercises designed to help you externalize your thoughts and feelings by becoming the observer. This is a critical skill that enables you to get off the bus and reduce the duration, frequency and intensity of repetitive thoughts and feelings. Sometimes just noticing them as "external" allows you to accept their occurrence, enabling you to refocus on productive activity and living your life.

Remember attempting to stop the buses from coming is counterproductive. Repetitive thoughts and feelings will come and may even increase by trying to stop them. Escape is not a solution because it entails distraction from the bus, which will still be on your mind if escape is the only purpose. Instead, seek out valued activity on which to focus. This will lead to a healthy and productive life and will get you off the bus.

Recall times when you suffered repetitive thoughts and emotions but then departed the bus by engaging in productive activities in your life. Even though you did not like the repetitive thoughts and feelings, you accepted they were there and, in spite of them, engaged in your life anyway. You did not try to rid yourself of the thoughts and

---

[1] Matthew A. Killingsworth and Daniel T. Gilbert, "A Wandering Mind Is an Unhappy Mind," *Science* Vol. 330, No. 6006 (2010): 932.

Get Off the Bus

feelings, nor did you think it possible to wish them away, or wait for them to go away. Instead, you reengaged in your life.

Repetitive thoughts and emotions overtake you in the same manner as portrayed in *A Nightmare on Elm Street*. Remember how the horrifying character Freddie Krueger could only get you and hurt you if you stopped paying attention to your life activities and focused on him? Freddie never really went away, just like thinking and feeling never go away. But focusing elsewhere on living one's life rendered Freddie harmless.

Achieving Present Focus

In our evolved state, humans have the capacity for introspective thinking. Introspection can challenge the brain's original purpose to help you survive. In other words, when your brain wanders inward to its own thoughts and feelings, it can also be moving away from its basic survival functions: to plan, to solve problems, to learn new things, to build, to create and to be aware of present external circumstances to enhance life and avoid death. When your brain is engaged planning, building and learning it is functioning in an optimal way.

Throughout this book you will learn how present focus is a crucial aspect of getting off the bus and back into life. Present focus occurs when you concentrate on something other than the stream of thought or emotion in your mind.

Present focus is a skill that can be developed. What can you do to develop your ability to focus on your present experience? This question will be discussed within the context of real-life examples in the chapters that follow.

To demonstrate a routine experience of present focus, I invite the reader to find an enjoyable snack. A piece of candy, a raisin, or a grape will work fine for our purposes. If it is bigger, just cut off a small piece.

Wait a second!

If you already ate the bite then you were not practicing present focus. You were not intensely concentrating on your experience. You might have been on the bus, eating your food on autopilot. If you were, go ahead and grab another piece and then proceed.

Without biting down on the snack, place it in your mouth, on your tongue. Notice its distinct taste. Roll it around in your mouth. Pay attention to its texture. Now chew it deliberately, slowly, using your whole mouth. Notice any bursts of flavor. Notice the sensation as you begin to swallow—continue to taste it all the while. Do you need to swallow more than once? Savor each aspect of your experience, fully enjoying it.

When you achieve present focus, you are fully focused and engaged. You are concentrating and your attention is focused on the present. You are off the bus. When present focus is achieved, you will find yourself slipping out of the grips of depressing thoughts and anxiety-provoking feelings.

When you experience negative thinking resulting in a depressed mood, you lose focus on your immediate environment. You may eat a meal you without actually experiencing a single bite. Far from savoring sensations of taste, you might be too busy dwelling on negative thoughts and feelings. When this happens, you automatically make a meal and eat it without tasting the flavors, the texture, or the sensations produced by combined ingredients. Continual attention to pessimistic thoughts can cause you to be overrun by gloomy feelings that rob you of your present experience, preventing you from enjoying the richness attainable in life. In contrast, full engagement in the present serves to bring you peace of mind and satisfaction. Present focus leaves fewer opportunities for dwelling on unproductive thoughts and emotions. Learning to accept and appreciate what life offers you will help you focus on the present, which will help lead you to healthy mental activity, which in turn will lead you to a more satisfying life.

To get off the bus, you must create a menu of healthy and engaging activities, all of which should be conducive to the values entailed by your life plan discussed below. The menu may include work, learning and any other experiences that require focus and concentration. These will all help to expand your awareness and foster your ability to focus on the present. One's ability to intensely focus on daily activities is developed with practice. Intense focus—even on routine activities like cleaning, chopping vegetables, or eating a sandwich—can reduce the frequency and duration of your bus rides. Intense present focus provides a richer experience in life. It also reduces one's tendency to dwell on neurotic thoughts and any attendant emotions. Think of engagement and intense focus as pursuits made while off the bus, which lead to mental health, clarity and overall satisfaction in life.

Creating Your Life Plan

People who have overcome regular experiences of depression, anxiety and self-doubt are generally those who have first identified and then applied their values to a long-term course of action—a life plan. Have you figured out what you truly value? Is what you value different than what your friends or family value? Remember not to let this question turn into a bus ride. Meaningful questions concern what *you* value, and whether or not the life you are living matches your values. Confident answers to these questions—or lack thereof—often correlate with the frequency to which one is on the bus.

Many people settle for lives that are not a reflection of their values. Although paths of least resistance may initially seem like the "easy way," they often lead one to later suffer resentment and regret. Among other things, your values may be reflected in spiritual participation; hard work; service to others; financial stability; participation in sports or hobbies; maintaining friendships; helping children, grandchildren or parents; finding and maintaining a romantic relationship or intellectual pursuits, such as obtaining more education, knowledge or understanding.

Action plans which offer an experience of values, such as those listed above, are developed to constitute a life plan, which may be thought of in terms of a blueprint: a big-picture plan for your life. This blueprint can help you make decisions both big and small. With your life's intended actions laid out, you are equipped with a course to follow. This course is not set in stone and can be altered as needed. Indeed, it is natural that changes will occur as you learn, adapt, and grow. All the while, the life plan purpose remains to organize your life according to values.

Take a moment to write down your values. Make a list, as it will help you organize your ideas. Include things like honesty, hard work, learning, having friends, spirituality, punctuality, kindness, generosity—of course, be sure what you write reflects what *you* really value.

After you have listed your values, take a moment to think about the activities that reflect your values. Consider the extent to which these activities are expressions of the values previously written.

Now make a list of five desirable and valued activities that you do or have done that make repetitive thinking and emotion almost impossible. These activities might include skiing or snowboarding on a challenging slope, or learning to play a song on a musical instrument.

Many people will write down activities like spending more quality time with family and friends; finding a more rewarding job; making new friends; perhaps doing volunteer work. What is on your list?

Now break out a big calendar if one is available. Sometimes smart phones do not provide the intended visual effect. With your calendar before you, write down the time, place and date you will engage in a few of the activities that most reflect your values. This is the action plan. With your plan right there in the ink detailing future events, you are taking a big step toward living your life plan.

In *The Wizard of Oz*, Dorothy clicks her red shoes together to transport her from Oz to Kansas. Unfortunately, life does not afford us special magic shoes with which to actualize our desires. We are however made with the potential to become the observer, to be aware of the destructive excesses of riding the bus, to identify the unproductive nature of repetitive thinking and feeling and to exercise present focus in whatever we do. From using these key skills we can depart the bus and live our life plan.

I personally struggled to stay motivated in graduate school. I also struggled to keep off extra pounds. Like anyone, the unproductive force of repetitively thinking caused me considerable distraction and suffering. These thoughts caused me to lose sight of my values and life plan and caused me to procrastinate, adding further to my struggles.

In particular, I struggled with questions concerning my schedule: On what and when would I work and study? What food would I eat and when? When and what kind of exercise would I commit to do? Not only answering, but following through with my answers to these questions ultimately released me from the struggle and suffering of irresolution. The realization of my values followed.

This led me first to change my environment. In so doing, I ensured I would not easily drift back into counter-productive habits of mind or activity, like distracting thoughts and eating on autopilot. I removed high calorie, high sugar drinks and food from my residence. I scheduled time in the library. I called a friend to join me at workouts. In the library and gym I was safe from bus rides.

My plan attended to each problem I identified, replacing them with actions that reflected my values. The extra pounds, the lack of focus and the want of motivation—all were resolved.

Another example of how a life plan can work is shown in the case of a single mother who wants to find an emotionally and financially stable partner. This goal reflects what she valued and would become part of her life plan. However to reach her goal she had to depart her buses, her repetitive thinking about her fatigue, loneliness and self-doubt, in order to pursue a course more likely to actualize what she valued. Her plan included joining a co-ed weekend hiking group, volunteering in a parent-child community project, participating at a place of worship with single men and talking to co-workers who may know a potential partner in the form of a friend or relative. Any of these options stood miles above hitting the bar scene to socialize because the men she was likely to meet outside the bar who were engaged in similar interests would be men who had similar values.

Her plan was a better course of action than attending the bar scene. Living life on the "wrong course" would no doubt set her up for more frequent bouts of disappointment, depression, loneliness, hopelessness and despair. These experiences are inevitable when you meet people who, while they claim to match your values, lack the life plan and initiative with which to deliver.

During her quest for a partner, she maintained and even gained friendships. Indeed, a life plan derived from your values provides you with many opportunities. It also helps you engage in present focus, which reduces repetitive thoughts and detrimental emotions. A life plan that reflects what you value offers you the building blocks for peace, satisfaction, and joy—as well as, and perhaps most significantly, reduced suffering.

A firm foundation for these building blocks requires social support. Social support arrives in many forms. Examples include social support from friends, from one's involvement with a community, or from the support offered by religious organizations. In counseling, there is also a form of support called the therapeutic alliance. Social support and the therapeutic alliance provide a stable foundation on which to construct and apply a life plan.

Social Support and the Therapeutic Alliance

Did you know that people who have social support are more resilient and stable in their mental and physical health? Research shows that social support offers what is called a "stress buffer" that provides resiliency in one's mental and physical health. In psychotherapy and counseling, a source of support emerges in what is called the therapeutic alliance. The therapeutic alliance refers to the positive, supportive relationship a person experiences with their therapist. This positive alliance between therapist and client is a form of social support. Without a therapeutic alliance, improvement in mental health rarely occurs. Numerous research studies show that the therapeutic alliance is key and accounts for most of the positive changes achieved in successful counseling.

If you are riding the bus, it is important to surround yourself with supportive people. When this is not possible, you will likely require a counselor or a psychologist to help. However, a supportive friend, acquaintance or therapist will only be helpful if you respect them *and* if their support moves you away from your buses. These individuals must be able to support you to get off the bus, rather than merely boarding them with you through endless discussions of your pain. Examples of informal support helping you get off the bus include a friend inviting you to join them to participate in an engaging hobby, recreational activity, social event or conversation.

Time spent with friends who stay off the bus has the benefit of keeping you from the bus. Remember that social support is a stress buffer that provides improved physical and emotional health. Making and keeping supportive friends with whom you have positive experiences deserves a place at the top of your priorities. A little proactive work in this regard can go a long way toward reduced suffering and a satisfying life.

I invite you to take a moment to do a friend inventory. This may seem an odd exercise, but it can be instructive. This exercise allows you to consider each friend's influence in relation to your values and life plan. Write down each friend's name, and then list your favorite pastime that you enjoy with each friend. Next consider whether these pastimes correlate with your values. Do the pastimes also match your life plan? Consider some other questions as well: Are the pastimes an engaging opportunity to relieve stress and get off the bus? Do you talk about problems but not solutions with this friend? Do you or your friend complain about life whenever you get together? Does this friend communicate in a way that makes you feel less adequate or more adequate?

Some readers may not have a friend nearby. You may have just relocated, or you may have just divorced and "couple friends" have disappeared. You may have even been riding the bus for so long that you have lost touch with your friends. You might repeatedly ask yourself, *Who would want to be my friend?* You may think, *I'm such a downer—no one would like a loser like me.* Recognize these thoughts as bus rides. These bus rides will not help you find friends. Find somewhere to volunteer your time. Meet people. Even though you feel terrible and nervous, talk. Vocalize your interests. Find common ground with those around you. You may surprise yourself.

Whether or not you have friends, it is helpful to get a counselor or a therapist. You might think of this person as a substitute friend equipped with a special playbook for life. As with friends, considerations concerning the quality of the therapist or counselor are important. Ask yourself these questions: Do you respect the therapist? Do you like the therapist? Do you focus on problems and solutions when you talk to the therapist? Do you feel better after meeting the therapist? Do you want to try new things after seeing your therapist? Do you talk about your buses, your suffering and your history of suffering? Does your therapist talk with you about what you want in life, your values? Does your therapist help you identify options that help you off the bus and into life?

If you like your therapist but do not make progress, do not be afraid to raise this concern with the therapist. Many people decide against expressing concerns *about* their therapy or therapist *with* their therapist, because they do not want to disappoint their therapist. This self-defeating course is quite the double-decker bus ride.

Finally, remember that no one is immune from bus rides. Friends get into ruts and have their own bus rides to overcome. At these times apply and share the tools you have learned from this book. Help others become the observer of the bus, develop awareness and present focus and discuss

Get Off the Bus

values and life plans. Use the bus metaphor to help you both stay focused and engaged.

Consider getting involved with group activities that have been proven to reduce emotional distress, such as yoga and meditation. Involvement with yoga and meditation groups will help you develop your ability to be the observer and experience present focus, as well as helping you build resiliency through social support. On top of these benefits, yoga and meditation groups may help you discover what you truly value.

If you find yourself reluctant, join a yoga or meditation class if only for the experience. If not yoga or meditation, find something that fits your interests. Participation in a hobby, a class or recreational activity with others will serve you well. Beyond this, consider finding a good therapist who moves quickly to help you get off the bus and into your life.

Magical Metaphors

The *riding the bus* metaphor has had enormous appeal to my friends, clients, and colleagues. It has been used to help many externalize their thoughts and feelings to become the observer. It is an effective tool that helps one recognize unhealthy patterns of emotion and thought.

As discussed, riding the bus occurs whenever you are churning or dwelling on thoughts and emotions that prevent present focus, thereby hindering peace of mind, satisfaction and progression toward your life plan goals. Use the bus metaphor to help remind yourself to actively focus on the present. Once you notice that you are riding the bus, name it or label it (e.g. "there's the angry bus"). When you assign a name to your bus rides, you will be able to identify them more readily and this will allow you to consciously focus on something more productive.

Many who have applied the bus metaphor have found it helpful to assign color labels to their various buses. Those with anger issues and resentful thoughts often refer to *their* bus as a red bus. "I was riding the red bus a bit too much last week," clients have reported. Other clients describe their buses as black or blue to label depressive or hopeless thoughts and feelings. For some, labeling the buses provides an effective reminder to become the observer of the bus and to stay off the bus in order to develop present focus and a life plan.

Some people do not find color-labeling their buses to be meaningful. If you are similarly inclined, continue to call the buses by descriptive names—the anger bus or the guilt bus, for instance. In any case, use the labels that are most comfortable and effective for you.

Presented below are definitions of common color-labeled buses, followed by more descriptively labeled buses and other metaphorical labels. Apply the metaphors that resonate best with you.

The Black Bus: This labels distinctive feelings and thoughts associated with suicide and not wanting to live.

The Blue Bus: This labels experiences of sadness, depression, hopelessness, low self-esteem and a lack of energy.

The Grey Bus: This labels the thoughts, feelings, and behaviors associated with procrastination or indecision.

The Purple Bus: This labels the feelings and thoughts associated with anxiety, worry, and panic.

The Red bus: This provides a label for emotions and thoughts related to anger, resentment, irritation, or all three of these emotions.

The Yellow Bus (or the Sunshine Bus): This labels fantasizing or picturing positive outcomes that may create positive, euphoric feelings. Yellow bus feelings, however, are not derived from actual life events and do not endure. For this reason, negative bus transfers frequently follow yellow buses.

The Bus Stop: This phrase is used to describe when one is conscious of approaching buses.

The Bus Terminal: This phrase describes an ongoing situation in which one takes a variety of bus rides without ever fully engaging in life. Each bus ride is followed with a period of idling, then a different bus ride is taken—and this cycle repeats. The person never fully engages in present life situations.

Bus Transfers: This is the descriptive label of replacing one bus ride with another. For example, this could describe ruminating on anxiety and fear, and then transferring to focus on depressed and hopeless feelings. Instead of engaging in life and disembarking the bus, one transfers to another.

The Double Decker Bus: This describes the experience of someone who is simultaneously on more than one bus. For example, I recall one client explaining, "I want to be fit and lose weight. I think about it a lot. It depresses me. But if I exercise and fill the home with better food choices, I feel so guilty that I am not taking care of my home or children and what they want."

The Greyhound Bus: This describes thoughts and feelings associated with past traumatic experiences. These are long distance bus rides with multiple emotions and thoughts associated with traumatic occurrences, such as child abuse, rape, and other memories of violence and trauma.

Tour Bus: The tour bus labels the process of exploring options but never fully implementing or engaging in any of them.

What names do you think could be used to describe the buses you ride? How can you begin to apply these metaphors into your life? In what follows I will relate these metaphors to those who have participated in therapy with me, who have effectively adopted them for personal use to facilitate progress in their lives.

Chapter 4

Anxiety and Panic

"Concentration is a fine antidote to anxiety."

— Jack Nicklaus

In the therapy sessions presented below, readers will observe how keys discussed come together to produce emotional and physical health. As you read these in-session interactions, watch for the therapeutic alliance to develop. Therapists facilitate this development through support, care and respect for the client. The clients in these interactions exhibit a variety of symptoms including depression and anxiety. Attending to these issues, notice the therapeutic strength created by the use of the metaphor to get off the bus.

Before moving to the in-session interactions, contemplate a few personal questions: When was the last time you worried yourself sick? How much of your day is occupied with worries about your finances? Has anxiety, fear, or panic ever stopped you from doing something important?

Even those who take medication for anxiety can still find themselves stuck in cycles of repetitive thoughts—riding the bus. In severe cases, individuals experience self-perpetuating anxiety, a dangerous cycle in which anxiety itself causes even more anxiety, stress, and worry.

Identify the keys that help clients free themselves from the bus in the therapist-client dialogues below. Pay attention to the methods through which clients become the observer, resolve repetitive thinking, focus on the present and benefit from social support and the therapeutic alliance, all while applying metaphorical bus labels. After you have observed how these keys actually operate, try to apply them yourself.

In this first therapist-client dialogue, Robert is sick with anxiety, stress and worry. Challenges presented by his new boss at work precipitate his distressed condition. Notice the keys that help Robert get back into a productive life.

Work Stress Leading to Anxiety, Depression and Low Self-Esteem

Robert entered the office for the first time. He spoke in a quiet voice. He explained that his doctor recommended he seek help in therapy.

Therapist: So how can I help you today?

Robert: I need help making a decision that is troubling me. I'm not sure if I should stay at my current job. I've had health problems lately. My doctor thinks a lot of my medical problems are stress-related and caused by my job.

Therapist: Robert, how is stress affecting you?

Robert: I am tired all the time. I sleep a lot. I sleep a lot during the day at home.

Therapist: What seems to be stressing you out the most?

Robert: My work. I'm not sure if I want to stay at my job anymore. I could probably retire. I've been there for over twenty years.

Therapist: What causes you stress at work?

Robert: I have a new boss. I used to be his boss—but since he took over, I've been angry and frustrated at how he mistreats people, and especially how he mistreats me.

Therapist: Do you think he's trying to get rid of you, Robert? Do you think you threaten him?

Robert: Uh, I don't think he's threatened by me. But yes, I think he's trying to drive me out. It's making me crazy. All I think about is him—how he's doing things, how he operates.

Therapist: Tell me more, Robert. I can see that thinking about your boss is eating you up.

Robert: Well, he was recently on my case because I was assigned to document the lack of progress by another employee whom he wanted to terminate. I didn't like how harsh my boss was regarding this employee.

Therapist: Harsh? How was he harsh?

Robert: He didn't really talk to him about his personal life or anything that might be interfering with his performance. He just simply wanted me to let him know all the things that needed to be improved, and he depended on me to put those things in writing.

Therapist: So he focused only on job performance with this individual?

Robert: Yes. My boss focused on missed deadlines and the failure to advise him when those deadlines were not met.

At this point, Robert reached into his briefcase and produced a twenty-five-page document putting the employee on official probation.

Therapist: So, Robert, did you prepare this document?

Robert: Yes, I did.

Therapist: It seems quite detailed and substantial.

Robert: Yeah, it is—but my boss got on my case frequently because he wanted it completed a lot sooner than when I got it to him. So toward the end, he wrote me up for missing the deadlines for the other guy's performance report! After that, I got really depressed and really nervous and paranoid about my job. I couldn't sleep at night. I'm having a great deal of difficulty concentrating at work and keeping my energy up.

Therapist: What do you think about your boss, Robert?

Robert: I don't know what to think. I just don't think he's a people person. How he demands things really bothers me. I'm not sure if I can cope with that kind of thing anymore. I dread the thought of staying there another five years. My medical doctor is putting me on a reduced schedule, but he says he will sign me out of work if I get too stressed out.

Therapist: When you think about work, Robert, when you think about your boss and how he works, what thoughts go through your mind?

Robert: Well, I think he's got it in for me, and he doesn't want me around. He never even says, "Hello," or, "Good morning." I'm pretty sure he wants me out. To tell you the truth, I get so sick thinking of him that retiring early is sounding better and better every day.

Therapist: You are fearful and worried that your boss may fire you. It frustrates and angers you because he doesn't show much personal interest or compassion to you or the other people in your office. Is that right?

Robert: That's right. I worry all the time then I get tired, lose my energy, and sleep all day on my days off.

Therapist: Robert, if I can help you stop stressing about work and about your boss, in spite of his style and personality differences, would that be of value to you?

Robert: That would be great, but I don't know how this works. How do we change him?

Therapist: Well, changing him might not be the answer. Changing how you think and reducing your stress over how he behaves may be more of the goal that I had in mind. I want you to think about coming in for a few sessions to try some ideas out.

My view of you, Robert, is that you have been a competent and loyal employee. You have been working for your company for over twenty years, and you have also been the boss there—and as I see it, that counts for something. You've endured the test of time. You've produced results over a long period. You're a "keeper." So it seems to me that you are thinking way too much about your current boss. You're thinking and making assumptions about how your boss is judging you. You're stressing yourself with negative thoughts so much it is interfering with your performance at work and making you feel sick.

In the therapist's statements above, the therapeutic alliance is strengthened as the therapist validates Robert, who is struggling to maintain a positive identity and a sense of power at work. Such validation from friends, family or a counselor is critical to a person who is trying to get off the bus.

Robert: Well, that about nails it. I'm basically paranoid and stressed out because I don't ever seem to do anything that pleases him. I've never heard him say "Thank you" or give a compliment—ever.

Therapist: Robert, that being the case, it's going to be very challenging for you to work with me on managing your stress. Your thinking, emotions, and what you focus on at work are all going to need to be addressed in our meetings. Are you in?

Robert: Sure, I'm in. You seem to know what you're doing. Dr. Burns, my family physician, speaks very highly of you.

Therapist: Robert, often when I work with someone who is experiencing a lot of stress, anxiety, worry, fatigue and depression, I notice that they spend a lot of time thinking. In your case, you think a lot about your boss and his potentially malevolent intentions. These may or may not be true. In fact, this is an assumption on your part. You are assuming that he is out to terminate you. There is no doubt this interferes

Get Off the Bus

with your concentration at work. So, I have a question for you: If you were not tormented by obsessive or recurring thoughts about your boss, how would you feel?

Robert: Doc, I would feel great. That's the whole problem. I can't stop thinking about him. It's making me sick. I can't turn off my mind.

Therapist: So, your mind just keeps going and going. Okay Robert, I'm getting a better understanding of this and I'm confident I can help you. But first, in order to have a common language between the two of us, I'd like to refer to a metaphor I like to use, an analogy for the type of repetitive thinking and feeling this situation is causing you. I call it riding the bus. Whenever one of my clients is making him or herself sick by excessive thinking or emoting, I like to refer to this as riding the bus. So if I say, *Robert, you're on the bus,* it means you're obsessively thinking about the things that you probably can't control—or things about which you are making assumptions, leading to paranoia, stress, fatigue and depression.

Robert: Okay, I've never thought of it that way. I may need to pack a lunch for the bus ride, 'cause I'm on that bus all the time!

Therapist: That's funny! But Robert, I want you to know that it's normal to think exactly as you've been thinking during this situation. Most people would think and react exactly the same way. However, it's still problematic. In other words, just because it's a normal reaction, doesn't mean that it's good for you. It just means that most people would be thinking the same way. Your work here with me will hopefully turn things around for you. The goal here will be for you to begin thinking and emoting far less about your boss and work situation. It is time for you to begin living far more both at work and at home.

Robert: I'm in. What's next?

Therapist: First, when you find yourself thinking about your boss actively observe these thoughts as they are: a bus ride— and don't get on for the ride. Or, if you catch yourself ruminating already then consciously get off the bus. Just because the boss bus pulls up and the door opens doesn't mean you have to board. When you are aware of these thoughts, you separate yourself from them. You become an observer of your thoughts. This helps reduce their impact on you.

Robert: Ok, I can do that. But what if the bus keeps coming back?

Therapist: There are ways to reduce your bus rides. If you are at home, concentrate on doing something productive. If you are driving and the bus pulls up in your mind, focus intently on your driving—don't get on the bus.

Riding the bus robs you of the experience of living. Riding the bus robs your attention from whatever you're doing. Riding the bus robs you of satisfaction in life. So be aware of when the bus pulls up to ensure you don't get on. Notice your worries and thoughts coming to you as intruders that only take from your attentiveness.

The second thing I want you to do is review exactly what your boss desires from his employees. I've had a lot of experience counseling executives from large corporations. I sometimes have a different view of what may make your workplace and your boss tick.

Robert: You do? Like what?

Therapist: When I listen to your stories about your boss, all of your stories demonstrate how uncaring and critical your boss comes across. In each of the instances that you bring up a common theme recurs.

Robert: What is that?

Therapist: Deadlines. Your boss seems driven by deadlines. He is obsessed with deadlines. Please try to notice this over the next week. While you're attempting to stay off the bus, intensely doing more productive things at home and at work, take note of the role played by deadlines and how this may be of critical importance to your boss.

Robert returned to therapy the next week.

Therapist: Hi, Robert. What challenges did you bring in for our work today?

Robert: My doctor released me to go back to work on a limited schedule—thirty hours per week. So I went back to work. When I started, my boss said something about not blaming him for getting sick. Can you imagine that? Then he proceeded to talk to me about a project that needed to be completed. I had other projects that I wanted to get done, but I decided I should try to listen to what my boss had to say and get started on his new project. The deadline that he set caused me to work fifty hours the first week back—far beyond the thirty that my doctor recommended.

Therapist: Wow, that's a welcome back. Seems like your boss really depends on you. Were you able to stay off the bus?

Robert: Oh no, not exactly. I rode the bus for a while thinking that he was mean for requiring me to work more than my doctor recommended. I thought, once again, he was trying to set me up to fail so that he could fire me.

Therapist: Yes, Robert, that is definitely what we call riding the bus. You were buckled in and off for a ride. Were you ever able to get off the bus?

Robert: You know—I was able to, actually. I thought about what you said—about how my thinking was making me sick. I decided to totally set aside my other projects and focus one hundred percent on what the boss wanted me to get done. And I did it.

Therapist: What happened?

Robert: Well, I felt better. I didn't find myself thinking about my boss so much. I finished the project on Saturday afternoon and then I followed your advice. When I went home, I focused on preparing my garden to plant flowers. I did this instead of obsessing about my boss and his potential intentions.

Therapist: That's great Robert. That's what I call present focus. It is very important to the goal of reducing the bus rides.

Robert: It was difficult to do at first. But I stuck with it. Then I got into it.

Therapist: What happened when you returned to work on Monday?

Robert: Nothing. My boss didn't even mention the project—didn't thank me for anything.

Therapist: Did he pick apart your report? Criticize it unfairly?

Robert: No, nothing. Didn't even mention it.

Therapist: Good. It appears your boss focuses solely on himself and his deadlines. That's it. Meet the deadlines and stay off the bus.

Robert: You know, for the first time I experienced more energy at home, too. I didn't feel like sleeping all weekend to recover from my thinking and worry.

Therapist: Robert, sometimes when people ride the bus a lot, it drives them "crazy." It's exhausting. It's stressful. In our times, and we observe it so often in our society—people do not really ever get off the bus. They turn to addictive patterns of behavior to distract and dull the ride. Many do things like sleep excessively or abuse drugs. Some people waste hours on video games and obsess over social media—some even view pornography attempting to evade the bus. Importantly, however, these habits constitute bus rides in their own right. These addictive patterns never lead to a resolution of one's problems. They never lead to making one's life better. In fact, in these cases many people never leave the bus terminal at all. They're always on the bus or, turning to their addiction, about to board another.

Robert, you now understand this. You've been able to gain the advantage of knowing what it is like to be off the bus and to be engaged in your life. You've experienced the power of separating yourself for significant periods of time from your repetitive thinking, separating yourself from both your thinking and your emotions that were making you sick. You've been able to become the observer of the bus and you

Get Off the Bus

have been able to engage in present focus. This has allowed you to focus on living. Living in the present moment brings you peace, satisfaction and joy.

Robert: Doc, it's so true. It's hard to believe how much better I feel already. I've been dealing with this problem for months and months. Now, in such a short time, I'm not always thinking that at any moment I'll be fired. Feeling that fear, feeling that anger, and feeling resentment toward my boss is not occupying my attention. I'm able to focus on what I'm doing rather than focusing on what I presume my boss to be thinking—which, by the way, I could never really know.

Robert continued in therapy every other week for two months. His focus in therapy was effectively dealing with his boss by staying off the bus. But Robert still continued to have complaints about his boss and about work. As therapy sessions continued, we were able to discuss long-term goals.

Robert: I'm doing much better at coping now. I'm not riding the bus all the time—but I'm still not really excited about work.

Therapist: You once mentioned you were nearing retirement age. Do you have a plan—a life plan, in other words—for you, your family and for work?

Robert: No. What is a life plan?

Therapist: We've been pretty focused on your boss and how to best cope with that situation. But we haven't really talked about what you value the most and what valued experiences you want more of.

Robert: I see. I sometimes wonder—even now with things are going well at work—if I should stay, or maybe do something on my own.

Therapist: Your satisfaction and peace of mind depend on your awareness of what you value and your ability to plan and implement valued experiences into your life. What do you truly value and what experiences do you want to pursue?

Robert: You know, over the years I have focused mostly on work. But now I want to spend more time with my wife, traveling a bit, spending time with my grandchildren.

Therapist: Do you have it scheduled on your calendar?

Robert: No. I've just been thinking about it.

Therapist: You know my philosophy, Robert. Thinking is overrated. Life is all in the doing—being one hundred percent engaged.

Robert: You are absolutely right. I need to talk to my wife and make plans. That way they happen and I'm not looking back regretting all that I didn't do.

Therapist: That's music to my ears. Robert; when would you like to come back in to review your life plan?

Two weeks later Robert returned for his scheduled appointment.

Therapist: Hi, Robert, how are you?

Robert: I'm doing well! That life plan thing we talked about was powerful.

Therapist: What do you mean?

Robert: Well, I went home and discussed the idea with my wife. We talked for hours. Now we just about have our entire life plotted out on the calendar.

Therapist: Wow. You guys really got into it and focused. What did you come up with? What are the highlights?

Robert: I suppose the biggest news is that I resigned yesterday.

Therapist: You what?

Robert: You heard right—I resigned. After discussing a life plan with my wife, I realized I wouldn't have the freedom to take off the time to do the things I wanted when I wanted to do them.

Get Off the Bus

Therapist: Are you scared? Worried about money at all?

Robert: That's a bus!

Therapist: Touché. You're right. So what are you going to do for cash?

Robert: I've always had consulting gigs. I'll just take on more of those when I want to.

Therapist: I've created a life machine here.

Robert: I feel so much better. I feel alive and excited about it all. I'm focused every day now on what I'm doing—you know, present focus, as few bus rides as possible.

Therapist: That is so great. You will find much more satisfaction, peace and joy, this way.

Robert's therapy continued periodically to address balancing his new work and home life. Looking back, he had no regrets about leaving his previous job. From time to time he would meet his co-workers for coffee. For a short time after these encounters he would experience resentment and briefly feel that sick feeling which led him to my office. He would then catch himself riding the bus and then focus on what he valued, planned-out activities with his wife, adult children and grandchildren. Robert maintained several friendships at his church, so social support was never a big problem for him. Three years later he is running a successful consulting business and enjoying what he values most.

Are you inadvertently putting off what you value in your life? In Robert's case, we saw how his presumptive thoughts about his boss's intentions to fire him consumed him, causing depression, anxiety and fear. Robert's example illustrates the common practice of creating one's own mental illness.

To turn things around, the therapist first developed a therapeutic alliance with Robert. Robert then learned to become the observer, to look at his own repetitive thoughts and worries as external intruders. To identify these thoughts, the bus metaphor helped Robert notice his anxiety, worry, and repetitive thinking. Next, we saw how Robert shifted from focusing on his mind—riding the bus—to engaging in his life at work and at home. This shift continued when Robert was able to identify his values. After his values were expressly stated, he was able to fully focus and engage in a life plan.

Think of situations that you avoid or make worse as a result of riding the bus. Do you ever resolve these situations? If not, what might help you resolve these situations? Contemplate what keys might help you resolve these situations in the future. If you find yourself putting off what you truly value in life, contemplate what proactive keys might assist you in changing your course.

Panic Attacks in Public Places

Once you experience a panic attack, which may include shortness of breath, heart palpitations, dizziness and sweats, your brain works extra hard to avoid ever experiencing another episode of panic. Unfortunately when you over-focus on not panicking and avoiding potential situations that you associate with the potential for panic, you make your anxiety worse.

The anxiety becomes worse as you constantly and repetitively think about avoiding the next panic episode. When you avoid normal situations because of a fear of having a panic attack your anxiety symptoms are actually reinforced because you experience temporary relief from the anxiety. Left untreated, panic can lead to a life that over time limits many places and activities that one requires or wants in order to lead a fulfilling life.

The relief you feel from avoiding situations reinforces your anxious aversion to the situation, so that the next time you are faced with the same situation you are even more likely to react with anxiety and attempt to escape it. Many people become emotionally and behaviorally trapped in this vicious cycle.

In the second therapist-client dialogue, Walter is suffering from debilitating panic attacks that took him almost completely out of normal life activities. Following the establishment of trust in a therapeutic alliance, Walter applies key steps to facilitate getting off the bus. This allows Walter to get back into normal functioning after his panic attacks.

We join Walter below during a follow-up session in which he discusses his suffering from panic attacks.

Therapist: Walter, where've you been? Good to see you.

Walter: Oh, just hanging out—and, you know, stuff for the holidays.

Therapist: What's it been—two months since you first came in?

Walter: Yeah. I probably should have come in sooner.

Therapist: So, what's up? What would you like to accomplish today?

Walter: Well, I'm still having problems.

Therapist: Tell me more about it. Refresh my memory. I remember that we talked about your riding the bus, but I forgot which buses you were riding.

Walter: Well, I tried applying the strategies you suggested to get off the bus. They sort of worked, but often I seemed to lose it. For instance, like, halfway through grocery shopping I would begin to intentionally panic and then I thought I might really pass out, so I would do whatever I could to get out of the store as soon as possible.

Therapist: Okay, now I remember. So you, after our first session, you went into stores with the intention of passing out. Is that right?

Walter: Right, remember, we tried the intention of panic stuff in-session. I felt relief when I tried to bring on panic or think about bringing on panic on purpose. It was weird. I did a one-eighty in my mind.

Therapist: Yes, it is weird how that works. It seems that once you accept and intend the panic, even the passing out, the brain stops overprotecting you, and you stop the repetitive thinking about how to avoid the situation.

If I recall correctly, your panic attacks started after you suffered from a prolonged bout of pneumonia.

Walter: Yeah, that's when it all started. About a week after I was sick, after I was strong enough to get back to work—the panic started.

Therapist: So, in some ways after our first consultation you were successful. You were able to intend the panic and the passing out. So for a time, at least, you were getting off the bus. Your intention allowed you to become the observer of your thoughts, which allowed you to work on them. Your intending the panic to occur is not your bus; your bus is wishing to escape the possibility of a panic attack at whatever cost.

Walter: On point. That's me.

Therapist: But you were able to achieve partial success and actually go into the stores that you had avoided prior to our first meeting.

Walter: That's right, but right in the middle of the store, after I was in there for about ten minutes, I would start to actually worry about having an attack. Then I would hurry out to my car and drive home.

Therapist: Yes, I remember we talked about the probability that your brain would shift right in the middle of your intention. I warned you about that particular bus—the oh-no-what-if-I-really-do-panic-and-pass-out bus. Apparently that bus came out of nowhere and you boarded without first observing it as such.

Walter: Exactly. That's exactly how it happened. I'm able to get off the bus, go into the store, intend my panic to come on—and then *boom*—it reverses on me and I think, *What if I panic and really do pass out?* Then I'm done.

Therapist: I'm sure I can help you through this, Walter. You're going to think it's weird but it will work. I am sure of it. Your past partial success constitutes considerable progress.

Walter: Okay, what's next? I'm game 'cause what I'm doing now isn't good. I stopped going into stores again and I don't hang out with my friends in public anymore. I haven't played basketball in three months, and I loved playing. I used to play four times a week before I got sick.

Therapist: We'll get you back into your life, Walter, especially into basketball. You know I love the game myself. We've got to get you back on the court.

Walter: That would be great. I really miss it.

Therapist: So tell me, when was the last time you played? And why did you stop playing?

Walter: It happened about a week or so after my pneumonia. I had just broken up with my girlfriend and I hadn't slept in a couple of nights. I wasn't eating. Then, I went and played ball in this league game. At a time out during the fourth quarter I couldn't remember anything—I couldn't even remember who I was playing with—nothing. I started talking nonsense for about two minutes. My friends were worried about me and I was embarrassed and scared. I haven't played ball since. I don't ever want that to happen again.

Therapist: But you do want to play ball again, right?

Walter: I do. For me, it was a great release—lots of fun and great exercise, too.

Therapist: Okay, so it's fair to say you are riding the panic bus when you begin to think about going to the store or going to play ball.

Walter: Yup.

Therapist: Okay, Walter. Remember the first step is to recognize the bus ride. Recognize your thoughts and your emotions as separate from you. They are going through you, and you are the observer of those thoughts and emotions. Each moment you spend in their grip is a moment of your life stolen away. Recognize that they are the bus and you don't have to ride, you don't have to focus on them. Though difficult, at times seemingly impossible, you can focus intensely on something else—your work, playing a musical instrument, cleaning, even playing ball—whatever you can do to keep yourself off the bus.

Walter: Cool. I think I get it. So how can I use this method better at the store?

Therapist: Good question. Let's go over the weird part first. Research shows that exposure is the best—perhaps the only—remedy for panic. Accordingly, I have some seemingly weird suggestions that follow from the research findings. They're actually similar to the suggestions that helped you get halfway through your shopping after our first session.

Walter: I'm okay with weird if it can help.

Therapist: Walter, after last session you scheduled your shopping, right? You got off the panic bus by intending to have a panic attack, while also concentrating on what you needed to buy at the store? That method engaged you in the present. It also stopped the repetitive thinking for a while. That worked for about half of the time it took to complete your shopping, right?

Walter: Right.

Therapist: This next week I want you to do the same—but plan ahead of time to purposely leave behind three items you want to buy. Stop your shopping before the halfway point, pay for the items, pack your car, and then go back into the store for the three items you didn't pick up. Remember your intention all the while to panic and pass out in the store. Do this two or three times—in the store, out to the car, then back in again.

Walter: It's funny because when I think of intending a panic attack and passing out, I can't help but laugh. It seems an impossible thing to do, which is relaxing. I get off the bus! I think this weird approach may actually work.

Therapist: You can do it. Don't expect perfection, but you will make progress by taking these steps. Remember, concentrate on the items you are after—their location, what they are, how they'll be used, how they taste, even. All the while, intend to panic.

Walter: I can do that.

Therapist: We also need to address the basketball situation.

Walter: Yeah. I really miss playing.

Therapist: Do you have a good friend that you play ball with?

Walter: Yeah.

Therapist: Does he know about your panic attacks?

Walter: Yes, I told him about it.

Therapist: Good. It sounds like he offers you social support. I want you to ask him to go play some one-on-one and shoot around one day. While you're there, apply the same strategy as in the store: I want you to intend to pass out as you're playing. Tell your friend about this plan so he knows. You may even share a hearty laugh about it together. His support will have a positive effect and, before you know it, you'll find yourself playing basketball off the bus.

Walter: Again, when I think about it, like, *Go ahead and pass out while I am playing ball with my friend*, the worry leaves me.

Therapist: Exactly. Walter, riding the bus for you is trying to escape the possibility of a panic attack. You've made good progress—you've done some good work today and have some good homework to try out over the next couple of weeks. Schedule up with me in ten to fourteen days.

The road may get bumpy and it may sometimes be a challenge, but the more you can stay off the bus through intentionally exposing yourself to the things you fear, the better off you will be—and the faster you will overcome this pesky bus ride.

Walter: Thanks! See you in a couple.

Therapist: You're welcome. Take care.

Walter returned to participate in several more counseling sessions. Each subsequent session, Walter became more confident engaging in situations that were previously aborted due to his panic.

Walter's counseling helped him understand that his panic was a function of his brain overprotecting him. The brain's biological purpose optimizes for survival. In evolutionary terms, most of survival entails avoidance of danger. So it is quite understandable that panic can become physically debilitating as repetitive thinking reinforces it.

Walter became the observer of the thoughts comprising his panic bus and, instead of directly trying to reduce them, he tried to consciously will them. This, of course, failed to produce any panic attacks, which allowed Walter to get off the bus. Walter was also able to shop by engaging in present focus. Using the same formula for success, Walter resolved the basketball conundrum with the social support of his friend. Notice that social support was present in each situation—in the store and on the court—through his therapeutic alliance and friendship, respectively.

What roadblocks in your life are created by anxiety, worry or panic? Can you think of past or present situations in which you could use any of the keys Walter applied to free himself from the jail his panic imposed? Don't be afraid to be creative—as we saw in Walter's case, sometimes seemingly weird solutions do the trick.

Panic Attacks When Driving

Peggy was a hardworking professional who was married with one child. She worked as a manager for a large department store. Over the past year, she had many absences due to a persistent sinus infection. Then, one day she experienced a panic attack while driving.

Peggy entered my office shaking, her head down.

Therapist: Please, take a seat. How did you find me?

Peggy: My insurance company referred me.

Therapist: Oh really, your insurance company?

Peggy: Yeah, the human resources person at work said you were on my insurance panel, so I called.

Therapist: Have you ever been in counseling before?

Peggy: No, I'm not really sure what to expect.

Therapist: Tell me, Peggy, what would you like to accomplish in counseling? What brings you here?

Peggy: I'm scared. I'm scared I won't be able to go back to work. And I'm worried I won't ever be able to take care of my baby on my own.

Therapist: Why these fears? What happened?

Peggy: Well, three weeks ago I was taken to the emergency room. I was driving to work and then I became dizzy and my heart started racing. I started to sweat. I felt like vomiting. I pulled over and called my husband. The dizziness would not stop and my heart continued racing. Finally, my husband took me to the emergency room. I was there for several hours. Since that time, I have not returned to work. I haven't dared to care for my son on my own. I'm constantly afraid I'll have another one of these attacks.

Therapist: Have you been physically ill or under a great deal of stress recently? Have you experienced loss of a loved one, starting a new job, surgery, or anything like that?

Peggy: No, no one in my family has died, but I've been very sick. I'm on my fourth round of antibiotics for a sinus infection. Nothing seems to cure it.

Therapist: What are your symptoms from the sinus infection?

Peggy: My head gets stuffed up, I get headaches, sometimes I get lightheaded, and I get tired by about three in the afternoon, generally.

Therapist: What occupies your mind during the day? You said that you're worried about having one of these attacks.

Peggy: Yes, I worry about losing control. I worry about passing out. I worry about becoming a danger to myself or to my son if I do pass out.

Therapist: How much do you worry?

Peggy: Since my panic attack, I worry constantly. From the time that I wake up, I have to have someone there with my son and me. After my husband goes to work, my sister comes over to make sure everything is okay. I even had to go on short-term disability from work.

Therapist: Are you taking any medications?

Peggy: Yes, sometimes. The hospital gave me some tranquilizers, but I don't like taking them. They make me too tired. I'd like to try to overcome this problem without medication, but I'm afraid. I'm afraid I won't ever be able to.

Therapist: Peggy, you're in luck because you've come to the right place. I'm confident that if you work hard on what I'm going to suggest to you, you will make progress. You will be able to go back to work, and you will be able to take care of your son on your own.

Peggy: Oh, that would be amazing. My husband is really getting tired of me not working and being so dependent on both his family and him.

Therapist: Peggy, your panic and dizziness seem to be generated by what I call a "sensitive brain." Your brain's focus is your body. It's focused on your body for a reason—you've been sick. You've been sick with a serious sinus infection for a long, long time. So long that your brain constantly pays very close attention to every change in your body. Your brain is doing this to protect you. Now, it seems to be overprotecting you. Your brain is especially sensitive to feelings in your head where your sinus infections have affected you the most. Then your brain focuses internally on your head. When this happens, it can actually create a sensation of dizziness. Once this dizziness starts, you then begin to worry about losing control—panicking and fainting, in other words. Am I on the right track, Peggy? Is this what you are experiencing?

Peggy: Yes, my heart starts racing and I start to feel dizzy and I worry I won't be safe.

Therapist: So worrying and thinking that you might pass out cause most of your panic? Is that correct?

Peggy: Yes, once I start thinking about it, I actually feel the dizziness coming on. As it gets worse, I just have to get away—I have to be by myself—I have to make sure that my son is being taken care of by someone else, either his dad or one of his aunts. If I'm driving, I definitely have to stop the car. I can't drive the car. After a while, the dizziness and panic goes away, but I still worry about it.

Therapist: Okay, Peggy. Right outside my office there are two bus stops. Buses go by here and stop every five minutes. Imagine that you, or your brain, are on the bus when you are worried about passing out due to dizziness. Let's say that you're on a bigger bus when you actually feel the anxiety, panic, and dizziness. This metaphor of riding the bus will be helpful for us to communicate about your panic. As weeks go by, you will learn how to get off the panic bus and back into living your life—without panic, without dizziness, and without anxiety. Did you know that gradually doing more and more of the things that make you panicky is the most effective way to get past the panic?

Peggy: That scares me.

Therapist: I know. It is scary. Your work with me to get off the bus will help you make progress. The first step is to focus intensely away from what your mind is delivering. Then we will take small steps to help you get your life back. This means we have to figure out how to first get you off the bus and second, how to get you to do things like be alone while you're taking care of your son and eventually, driving to work and working.

Peggy: So, you think this will help me?

Therapist: Yes, you will have to work at it, but it will help.

Peggy: I'm ready to work on it.

Therapist: This next week, I'd like you to do a couple of things differently. First, I want you to begin to consider thoughts of panic, worry, and collapsing—along with your actual panic and dizziness—as riding the bus. Accordingly, I want you to notice when the bus pulls up. This will help you take a step back and see the bus from an observer's perspective. In other words, see these thoughts externally as opposed to an overwhelming part of you. As you begin this process over the next week or so, you may notice that the bus pulls up frequently. At times you will lose track of this assignment, and you'll recognize that you are in the midst of a bus ride—already engrossed in thought, dwelling on your panic. When this happens, your goal is to get off the bus at the very next bus stop. Other times, notice the bus in the anxiety and panic, and the idea that pops into your head telling you that you can't go on. As you observe these thoughts, dissociate from them: they are the bus and you need not entertain them. Label them with what they represent, whether panic, fear, or any other form your bus takes. After you've done this, focus your attention on something productive like a hobby, an activity with friends, or a good book. Whatever else, don't dwell on the thoughts.

Peggy: How do I not dwell on them?

Therapist: To get off the bus you must learn to productively concentrate with one hundred percent focus. For example, pay one hundred percent attention to your son, to what he's doing, to what he's saying, and to what you'd like to teach him. Not the usual fifty percent or even seventy-five percent. Focus one hundred percent. This is what I call present focus, and it's a skill you can develop. While it helps you become more productive and healthy, it also keeps you off the bus. The worry bus will lead to repetitious thoughts about the dizziness you've experienced, going back to work, driving your car, or caring for your son on your own. This leads to the longer and more troubling emotional bus rides of anxiety and panic. On its own, feeling dizzy is not that bad. If you felt dizzy while you were driving, you'd simply pull over and wait for the dizziness to pass. You wouldn't give it much thought.

Peggy: That's amazing. So, it is actually *the thinking* about having dizziness that is making me feel sick?

Therapist: Yes, exactly. But I also believe you may sense that something is physically wrong. You've had a sinus infection for over four months. Your brain is overly sensitive to changes in how you feel. This provokes panic and panicky thinking. It provokes you to jump on and ride the bus.

Peggy: So how do I get past this? My doctor wants me to try one more round of a different antibiotic, but he's also talking about surgery. Now I'm thinking and panicking about the surgery!

Therapist: These are normal thoughts and feelings. They become abnormal when they take you away from living your life. It's really important that you begin to focus and concentrate on the things that you do in your life. And when you do these things you must focus intensely on what you're doing, concentrate one hundred percent. This is your goal.

Peggy: How can I do that? What do you mean?

Therapist: Well, first you must notice when a bus pulls up. That is when your negative thinking sets in. Then, you must concentrate one hundred percent on what you're doing, so that you aren't riding the bus—dwelling or obsessing on thoughts that make you panicked, sick or hopeless. If you're cleaning something—like the kitchen floor—don't let your mind wander and ride the bus. Clean with intensity, noticing each step, each swipe, each speck of dirt. Concentrate deeply on what you're doing. When you do this, you won't be on the bus; instead, you'll be in the present. This is the skill of present focus.

Peggy: What about my dizziness?

Therapist: Dizziness can be a bus, too. By focusing on internal feelings in your head, by focusing on and searching for internal sensations in your head—the site of your infection and dizziness—you can actually provoke your own dizziness. It's important that you stay externally focused. So, when you are tempted to focus inward on your physical condition, you must then deliberately focus outward, paying attention to external things. This external focus is a way of staying off the bus. Start using your five senses. Focus on the sensations they offer you. This focus will help you regain balance and it will help diminish any dizzy feelings.

The therapist counsels Peggy to be mindful and develop the skill of present focus. There are many books published on mindfulness and the benefits of being "present." They all promote their own methods of not riding the bus.

Peggy: Okay, I can try that. I will try that at home. Maybe I will push myself to take a walk alone—maybe even a drive around the block. I will intensely focus on my steps and my surroundings.

Therapist: That would be great, Peggy, but don't push yourself too hard. Right now, I'm mostly interested in your ability to notice when the bus pulls up. When those feelings arrive, be aware of them and then try to increase your ability to engage in something related to your life with one hundred percent concentration. These are important steps toward getting off the bus. Schedule with me early next week. Come in next week with some bus stories.

Peggy was seen in therapy on a weekly basis for about six weeks. During this time, she was able to progress back to normal functioning. However, without warning, during week six Peggy suffered a setback. She experienced a panic attack after her brother visited her home and talked about a cousin who was recently diagnosed with cancer. We join her below in her seventh session of therapy.

Get Off the Bus

Peggy: Am I ever going to get rid of this panic and dizziness? I thought I was better and then, *bam*. I wasn't able to drive. I wasn't able to take care of my son by myself. I was back where I started: panicked and dizzy. I couldn't even think about going back to work.

Therapist: Wow, that must have been a scary and disheartening experience. Somehow though, you did not go to the hospital. In a way, I'm glad you experienced this lapse at this time. Lapses—like the one you just had—are common and are even to be expected. In the time leading up to the lapse, how frequently were you checking for buses pulling up? How often were you being an observer of your thoughts?

Peggy: Oh—ah, well, I kind of stopped checking. I really didn't need to check for buses any longer. Everything was going fine. I was driving. I was taking care of my son without help. Then my brother came over and that did it. I was back at square one.

Therapist: First of all, it's normal to relax and become less aware of the buses. However, if you maintain conscious consideration of the buses—aware of when and where they are likely to pull up—you can avoid the ride by engaging in something else.

Peggy: I can try.

Therapist: Have you ever played a sport or musical instrument, Peggy?

Peggy: Yeah, I played volleyball in high school.

Therapist: Great. When you were into a game, would you be on the bus, thinking about yourself or the last game?

Peggy: No. I didn't think about much other than the ball, really.

Therapist: Exactly. Now think: Do you currently engage in any activities during which you reach a comparable state of mind to your focus in volleyball games?

Peggy: Well, sort of. I take a yoga class.

Therapist: Perfect. Yoga is an activity in which you focus one hundred percent on your pose and breathing. When you are into a yoga session, you cannot be riding the bus. So, your goal is to make yoga more of a routine activity in your life. Outside of yoga, work on developing one hundred percent focus in other activities. While doing so, be aware that panic buses will occasionally return to your bus stop. Peggy, when do you think those buses are most likely to return?

Peggy: Well, this time I was trapped on the bus after my brother told me about my cousin's cancer treatment. I guess whenever there is a conversation about someone else's experience that is similar to my own condition—or even my own illness—I'm at greater risk to ride the bus.

Therapist: Perfect. That's exactly right, Peggy. Remember, your brain is finely tuned to be sensitive to physical illness. You've been sick for several months.

After eight sessions of therapy, Peggy returned to her job full time. She was able to practice driving alone, starting with driving to work. Currently, Peggy follows up in therapy once every three to four weeks. Peggy's next challenge is physical and psychological recovery from sinus surgery. This surgery is likely to intensify the panic and dizziness buses associated with her thoughts about illness. However, going into surgery, Peggy is now prepared and she is planning to be aware of the buses. She will attempt to do something to keep her brain fully occupied in the present during her recovery period.

It's easy to see how Peggy's bus riding was triggered whenever she sensed anything related to her illness. Can you identify what triggers your bus rides? Maybe it's the way someone phrased a text message to you. Perhaps it's when someone blames something on you for which you are not responsible. Notice how your bus rides are composed of repetitive thoughts and negative emotions.

Worry and Panic about Physical Illness

In the next therapist-client dialogue, we meet Laura. She has experienced her first episode of extreme and debilitating anxiety and panic. Similar to Peggy, Laura did not experience any of these symptoms before her first episode. These episodes can be devastating when left untreated; beyond the immediate disruption they cause, they can turn out to be life altering.

Laura, age forty, was referred by her primary care physician for cognitive behavioral therapy. At the same time, her doctor administered medication therapy, including an antidepressant and a tranquilizer. Laura, a seventeen-year executive assistant at a large manufacturing firm, reported an unremarkable psychiatric history with no prior episodes of panic or anxiety.

We join Laura below near the beginning of her first session in which her condition is assessed.

Therapist: Have you ever seen a therapist before?

Laura: No. This is a first. I'm usually the one helping people solve their issues.

Therapist: What would you like to achieve by coming in to counseling?

Laura: I think I'm losing it. I'm constantly worried that I am or will be sick. I worry so much now that I feel everything in my body. I get panicked about aches and pains. I think they're the beginnings of diabetes.

Therapist: Why diabetes?

Laura: My dad had it. I'm still not over his death. It's been over a year, but I'm still sad.

Therapist: Your father's passing was an extremely emotional time for you, wasn't it?

Laura: Yes, he suffered with the diabetes. We were close. It was hard to watch my dad suffer.

Therapist: Have you worried about your health since his death, or has this concern been only more recently?

Laura: It has always been in the back of my mind, but about three months ago I became sick with the flu. Since that time, I have been a mess, always thinking about every ache or pain as if I have diabetes. I get panicky and sometimes dizzy. I'm afraid I'm going to pass out. I'm afraid of flying. I worry that I'll pass out in a restaurant. My husband wants to go out to dinner and I tell him that I can't go because I'm worried I'll get sick at the restaurant.

Therapist: This is really disrupting your life. Are there any other worries?

Laura: Yes—while I've cut my hours at work and avoided traveling, I can't avoid travelling for work forever. I've been growing with the company over the years and was recently promoted to an executive position. To keep my position, travel is required. I now am expected to travel nearly all the time. Before a trip I get sick with worry that the plane is going to crash. I won't even plan a vacation with my husband because I can't stop from thinking about the plane crashing.

Therapist: Are your symptoms occurring every day?

Laura: Yes, they come every day.

Therapist: When are they the worst?

Laura: After work in the evening. I can't get my mind off my aches and pains. I worry a lot about the next time I will have to fly for a work trip, and at night my mind races.

Therapist: When does the worry and panic seem to subside?

Laura: Mostly when I'm at work. When I'm in the middle of a work project my thoughts seem less intense.

Therapist: Good. I'm glad that you are able to notice the difference.

Laura: But I'm worried that I will need to quit my job.

Therapist: I know these thoughts and feelings are shocking. They make you feel out of control. You have a good history though, and there's no doubt you'll respond to counseling. It appears that your brain likes to solve problems. Your work history is outstanding. You take care of your busy family. This shows that you are a problem-solver. Your mind excels at figuring things out, making plans, and taking action. Recently, over the past few years, your brain has been paying more attention to your body—and now, it sounds like, even to your thoughts and feelings, which are endlessly repeating themselves. You pay attention to aches and pains, to what you think about them, to changes in how you feel. Your brain has become increasingly focused on what might be going on inside of you or what might happen to you.

Laura: You're right on. And I actually do much better when I am busy doing things—not worrying about what is going on inside me, you know?

Therapist: That's right. When your brain is focused externally on what you're doing, you experience fewer symptoms. That's what I call getting off the bus. And when you are worried, panicking, and focusing your thoughts on your aches and pains, that's what I call riding the bus. When you are riding the bus, you are sick with worry, rather than being focused on what you are doing.

Laura: What I don't understand is why I'm so sick with worry, why I'm so overwhelmed, or why I'm riding the bus.

Therapist: Laura, you've been through a lot: your father's diabetes, his suffering, and his death, followed by your sickness with the flu. These events have shifted your brain's focus to your body and to worrisome thoughts about your own mortality. Just realizing that this is what is happening is a good first step to getting off the bus. Your brain, in a way, is excessively sensitive and responds with overprotection. Once you have a disastrous thought, or notice a sensation in your body, you ride the bus. You begin to dwell on what might happen—getting diabetes, your plane crashing. These thoughts make you feel sick, overwhelmed, and panicky. These feelings spawn even more thinking about what might happen and how to avoid these things. Is that right?

The therapist checks in to ensure that he is on the right track with the client. If you are a client, be sure your therapist is on the right track for you.

Laura: That about describes it perfectly.

Therapist: Your brain needs to get off the bus and focus on what's in front of you, not inside of you. If you intently focus on what's in front of you, you'll be off the bus. Like you said: when you are engrossed in a work project, you aren't thinking about planes crashing or potential sickness.

Laura: So, how do I stay off the bus?

Therapist: Well, the first step is to realize that riding the bus means that your thoughts and feelings are caused by an overly sensitive brain. Second, to prevent the bus ride—or to get off the bus if you've already boarded—you will need to focus your brain's attention on what you are doing. You must direct your brain's attention to the present and away from the thoughts that are coming into your head. When you are focused one hundred percent on what you are doing, you will have gotten off the bus.

Laura: So I should focus my attention on what I'm doing, while trying not to think about my aches, pains, and worries?

Therapist: Not exactly. You see, Laura, you can't really stop the thoughts and feelings from coming. In fact, trying not to think about them can actually increase the thoughts and feelings. The goal is to focus more intensely on what you are doing and accept that the scary thoughts will come and then go.

Laura: So, how do you focus more intently on something else? My evenings at home are miserable.

Therapist: Focusing intently at home can begin with your children and husband. You know how you can pay partial attention—say, only thirty percent—yet still respond and reply to your husband and children? Instead, I would like you to focus one hundred percent to what they are saying. And when you respond, respond with one hundred percent of your effort.

Laura: Yeah, I do that thirty percent a lot. Sometimes it's only ten percent and my daughter yells at me to listen to her.

Therapist: Exactly. Staying off the bus when you are home requires listening to your husband and children with one hundred percent concentration. Sometimes "active listening"—that is, paraphrasing what others have said before you answer—is a good way to intensify your concentration on listening.

Laura: This won't be easy. I'm so used to the routine at home that my mind is always on the bus there.

Therapist: It will be challenging at first, but it's a skill; with practice you will become better and better at it. You may also increase your present focus, staying off the bus by focusing on a number of other routine things at home.

Laura: Like what?

Therapist: Well, you can focus more intently on things like preparing dinner. For example, very intently concentrating on cutting vegetables could help. Watch the knife slice through each vegetable. Pay attention to the size of the cuts, the texture you are cutting through, the amount you are cutting. You may typically do these things automatically without concentration. But now the goal is to give your brain something to intensely focus on in order to stay off the bus.

Laura: So, even the little things that you do—you mean to say you analyze them?

Therapist: You observe. You concentrate. You stay present. No good-bad or right-wrong judgment necessary.

Laura: Do you think this will work? I mean, you must think it will work—but it just seems so simple.

Therapist: It may seem simple, but it is a skill and it will take time to develop this skill. It will take time for you to catch yourself on the bus in order to get off of it sooner. It will take time to improve your concentration.

Laura: My doctor prescribed medications for me to take, but I really don't like taking medication. Should I take them?

Therapist: The medications are typically prescribed to help reduce your symptoms, to help your emotions and your thinking become less sticky, so to speak. It's your decision to begin taking them or to wait and see how you're able to get off the bus over the next couple of weeks. Let's schedule a follow up appointment in about four or five days. At that time, you can tell me stories you have of getting off the bus.

Laura progressed rapidly with her treatment. She attended five sessions of therapy and made considerable progress after each session. She began to view her symptoms—her thoughts and emotions—as passing buses.

During her third and fourth sessions, Laura complained about her inability to get off the bus while she was trying to fall asleep. During these sessions, the therapist demonstrated focused breathing exercises and advised Laura to apply the breathing exercises at bedtime. When engaged in focused breathing, you focus on the temperature of the air going in your nostrils, the feeling of your expanding abdomen, and the temperature of the air and the sensation of it going out your nostrils. As Laura practiced this, she reported back that her sleep improved. Later on in counseling, Laura addressed her grief issues.

Agitation and Stress Reactions in the Morning

Many people who suffer from negative thinking caused by stress and tension experience diminished energy, reductions in motivation, declining work performance and strained relationships.

Individuals who suffer with anxiety often report their symptoms are worse when they wake up, whether in the morning or in the middle of the night. This common occurrence is associated with dream sleep, which describes times when we are emotionally charged from our dreams. Most dreams generate full-blown physiological reactions. This, combined with an anxious personality, can create a worrisome condition. Mark, 45 years old, is presented next. He wakes up each morning with extreme tension.

We join Mark below at the beginning of his first session with the therapist.

Therapist: Hi Mark. How did you find me?

Mark: My family doctor recommended you.

Therapist: Oh, that's great. He's a good doc and a good person.

Mark: I really like him. He says you're the best.

Therapist: Oh no. That just raised the bar for me. What problem are you here to work on today?

Mark: I just don't feel like myself anymore. I'm constantly stressed out.

Therapist: What do you mean by stressed out? What are your feelings, your thoughts? When is it the worst? Does it ever get better?

Mark: It's probably the worst in the middle of the night and when I wake up. I don't have many thoughts when this starts. I just feel tense, very tense. I feel like I'm going to blow up any minute. Sometimes I'll feel stressed out, other times just plain agitated—but not ever about anything in particular.

Therapist: Are you getting a full night's rest?

Mark: No. It's difficult for me to fall asleep. My mind races and then when I do fall asleep, I wake up around three-thirty or four in the morning. Then I can't go back to sleep. That's when I feel the most tension and I get an amped-up feeling.

Therapist: Do you experience worry, negative thoughts, or make negative self-judgments when this occurs?

Mark: Not really. I just feel agitated, like I'm going to explode. Then I just continue to feel that way, more or less, for the rest of the day. I worry about why this feeling is happening.

Therapist: It seems that you start out each day early in the morning with a tremendous amount of tension. Many people who have high anxiety report that they experience the most severe symptoms of anxiety first thing in the morning. This is because you are just awakening from your dreams. When you dream, even though you are asleep, your brain is fully awake. As you know, dreams can create a great deal of tension, stress, anxiety, fear and that "amped up" feeling. It seems that you would benefit from "unplugging" from these feelings after you wake up in the morning.

Mark: Boy, that would be nice. When I wake up, I feel like I'm about to explode.

Therapist: As a way of separating yourself from these tense feelings, I would like to refer to your morning feelings of tension as riding the bus. The goal, then, in your counseling here with me, is to help you get off the bus.

Mark: Okay. How does that work?

Therapist: Well, research—along with hundreds of years of experience—shows that deliberate, focused, deep breathing quiets the mind and relaxes the body. I'd like you to try some of this breathing. Let's do some right now. I'd like you to focus all of your attention and concentrate one hundred percent on the air molecules entering your nostrils. Feel the air going in.

At this point, the therapist models the breathing.

Therapist: Breathe deeply. Feel the air expand your chest down to your belly. Then, after holding the air for a split second, focus on the air leaving your nostrils. Feel the

Get Off the Bus

warmth of your breath going through your nostrils. Try this slowly, again and again. Right now, do this deliberately. Focus on it intensely. I'll do the same. Let's practice this for the next few minutes.

Mark: Okay.

Mark slowly inhales and partially closes his eyes. After about three minutes and many inhalations later, the therapist starts back into discussion.

The therapist demonstrates the effort and explains that completely unplugging from the mind—being off the bus and staying focused on one's breathing—is a challenge for anyone. Modeling, practicing and receiving feedback are among the most powerful forms of learning.

Therapist: So let's talk about the breathing exercise. Were you able to focus one hundred percent on the breathing?

Mark: Well, most of the time. At first, my attention would go back to why I was here. Then I kept thinking about whether or not I was doing the breathing correctly. But I think I finally got into it and was able to exclusively focus on the breathing.

Therapist: Great, when you were concentrating one hundred percent on the breath, did you also think about your problems? Did you ride the bus when you were breathing?

Mark: No.

Therapist: When you were focused on your breathing, did you feel tense or amped up?

Mark: Actually, between breaths I noticed the intensity was much less.

Therapist: How about during the breaths?

Mark: I kind of blanked out on all feeling in the middle of it.

Therapist: Excellent, that means you were off the bus. So this next week, when you see or anticipate tension coming— when you see that tension bus pulling up to you, or if you discover you're already riding it—you must then immediately focus on breathing. This will help you get off the bus, if not avoid it altogether. If you're on the bus when you begin to do the breathing, it will at least slow the bus ride down, reducing the intensity of the ride so you can eventually get off the bus.

Mark: I will try that. But what about falling asleep? I'm having a terrible time falling asleep. Will this breathing help with that too?

Therapist: Focused breathing can be very helpful with sleep problems. As you said, when you try to fall asleep, your brain races from one thing to another, getting you amped up. Breathing exercises will give your brain something physical to focus on. Practice this method many times a day. Remember, you'll get better and better at doing this as you use it more and more often.

Mark attended a few more sessions. He made remarkable progress. He reduced his stress and anxiety reactions during the day and was able to use the breathing exercises to fall asleep. Developing his focused breathing, Mark was able to stay off the bus while he engaged more fully in his daily life. Over the course of three sessions spanning just three weeks, Mark was able to apply the breathing exercise and get off the bus most of the time. He continued to experience some intense feelings in the morning, but it bothered him less. He relied on the focused-breathing exercise to diminish these feelings of tension and then committed himself to focus on his day's activities.

Have you ever awoken after a full night's sleep only to feel exhausted or tense? Perhaps you were in intense dream sleep. How do you orient yourself? Do you stretch? Do you take deep breaths? Do you switch focus to your daily routine? Have you ever noticed how animals tend to stretch and take deep breaths when they first wake up? Maybe they can teach us something.

Using in-session dialogue, this chapter illustrated how anxiety and panic can seemingly come out of nowhere with debilitating results. The dialogue also demonstrated the steps one can take to counter the effects of bus rides to get back on track and resume a normal life.

Notice how clients became so stuck in thoughts and feelings that any resolution evaded them. Consider this occurrence in Laura's case:

Laura: So I should focus my attention on what I'm doing, while trying not to think about my aches, pains, and worries?

Therapist: Not exactly. You see, Laura, you can't really stop the thoughts and feelings from coming. In fact, trying not to think about them can actually increase the thoughts and feelings. The goal is to focus more intensely on what you are doing and accept that the scary thoughts will come and then go.

To stay off the bus as much as possible, Laura learned to focus more intensely on the present and fill her schedule with valued activities to focus on. She also learned to view her thoughts and emotions as external to her—as buses. This helped her resist temptation to dwell on her thoughts and feelings.

Therapist: You observe. You concentrate. You stay present. No good-bad or right-wrong judgment necessary.

Notice that the habit of making good/bad judgments about thoughts, feelings, and external experience exacerbates your dwelling on negative thoughts and feelings. It is a challenge just to focus on the present and be ready to focus on what comes next without a binary judgment of your external or internal experience.

Notice how thoughts and feelings associated with worry and fear tend to evoke these judgments, which only exacerbates their repetitiveness. As you go through your day, note how frequently you automatically judge physical and mental events. Notice how these judgments stick to you.

Try to consciously attend to these judgments for a few hours of your day—as you do, first accept that each one came to you. From this perspective, you are able to observe and label them. This frees you to then refocus on the present.

You will begin to notice a heaviness lift from you. Your ability to focus will improve. Your satisfaction and sense of peace will flourish.

It may seem curious that Jack Nicklaus, a professional golfer—and not a philosopher or psychologist—was quoted to introduce this chapter. "Concentration is a fine antidote to anxiety," he said. Taking this notion a step further, it is best that we embrace that there are no good shots or bad shots, only "the shot" you are taking now.

Chapter 5

Obsession

"Life isn't as serious as the mind makes it out to be."

— Eckhart Tolle

What happens when anxiety and the need for relief become more serious? Have you had days you can't get a certain thought out of your mind? Has it ever continued for weeks, even months? Obsessions have the potential power to take over a person's life, filling them full of sorrow, regret, grief, guilt and fear, among other things.

When obsessions occur, anxiety is created. Most people will go to great lengths to understand why their obsessions are occurring. Desperate for answers, many find themselves willing to try almost anything to rid themselves of their obsessions. But the more you focus on trying to rid them, the worse they get.

Regrets, Guilt and Grief

In the next therapist-client dialogue, we are introduced to Greg. His bus ride is obsessive thinking, and it is starting to dominate his time, decreasing his engagement in life. As you read the interaction between Greg and the therapist, try to relate Greg's experiences to times you have obsessed about something to the extent that it interfered with your life.

Previously, Greg had received therapy and medication for his depression and obsessive-compulsive tendencies. Greg, age 74, was undergoing a dialysis treatment at a city hospital three hundred miles away from his home. As such, he was facing many adjustment challenges to major life changes, including moving from his home to a senior living community without the option to drive a car. Greg's first eight sessions of counseling focused on his practical adjustment to being in a new city and a new home. Greg was active, fit, chatty and detailed when he spoke. Greg was anxious and obsessive about almost everything.

We join Greg at the beginning of one of his regularly scheduled sessions with the therapist.

Therapist: Hi, Greg. How are you doing this week?

Greg: Not so good. I've been having meltdowns.

Therapist: What do you mean by meltdowns?

Greg: I think about my life, all the changes, and I just breakdown and cry. I keep thinking that I have to do my grief work because if I don't then I will always be depressed.

Therapist: Grief work? What is the source of your grief, Greg?

Greg: My ex-wife. My previous therapist said I have to do grief work before I can move on and be happy. I keep thinking of that.

Therapist: When do thoughts about the grief work come to you?

Greg: All the time now. But mostly before I go to sleep and when I wake up in the morning. At night, it prevents me from sleeping. In the morning, I can't concentrate and I have trouble getting going. I feel exhausted.

Therapist: Greg, these thoughts are really disruptive and they are interfering with your life.

Greg: I know. I can't stop thinking about how I need to do the "grief work" because, if I don't, I will stay depressed. So I started going through the book my therapist recommended.

Therapist: Our work together here, Greg, is going to be different from your past therapy. Your past "grief work" cannot be your current "life work" if you seek peace and satisfaction in your future.

Greg: I'm not sure what you mean. My former therapist told me, and the book says it too, that I first have to grieve before I can move on and be happy.

Therapist: That may have been true when you were divorcing three years ago, but not now. We need to focus on a life plan. Let's call it "life work."

Greg: I don't know what you mean.

Therapist: Well, Greg, I'm worried that excessively focusing on "grief work" is leaving you too sad. When you become obsessed with the past, it takes away any opportunity for you to live your life now. In fact, Greg, the repeated thoughts informing you that "grief work" is necessary before you can be happy are no longer applicable. In your current state, these thoughts actually interfere with your peace of mind and satisfaction. I work with many who are stuck in cycles of grief, anger, regret and worry. My goal is to help my clients separate themselves from these kinds of thoughts and feelings about the past. When my clients focus on these troublesome thoughts and feelings, I call it riding the bus. So, I explain to my clients that our main goal in counseling will be to get off the bus and back into living life.

Greg: Okay. So how can I do that?

Therapist: Let's take a step back and talk about what you value, what you want to fill your life with, what brings you peace and satisfaction.

Greg: Well, ok—but how will that help?

Therapist: People often lose their direction. They lose sight of what is meaningful to them, of what's important to them. Articulating our values helps us reorient ourselves.

Greg: But a lot of what is important to me is gone now: my home, my chores on the ranch, my married life and that companionship.

Therapist: Exactly. So it's even more important to go over your values in order to identify what you can do *now* that will contribute to health, happiness, and satisfaction in your life moving forward.

Greg: I'm so sad.

Therapist: I know. Your focus has been on what you've lost, which results in sadness. Is there anything in your life that currently brings you peace and satisfaction? Any activities that you value now?

Greg: Yes. I like to help people. I'm always helping people who live in my retirement community.

Therapist: Good. That's what I mean. What else do you do?

Greg: I do volunteer work at my church and at the hospital.

Therapist: Perfect. These are meaningful. You are making a difference. Contributing. What else?

Greg: I read my bible every morning. My morning devotionals—I used to do these almost every morning. But with the meltdowns and thinking about my "grief work," I've not done much lately.

Therapist: You've lost some weight. Is being in better shape important to you?

Greg: Yes. I made it a priority.

Therapist: How did you feel about the weight loss?

Greg: I feel good about it. It's a priority in my life to be healthy.

Therapist: Good. So you value kindness and helping those less fortunate. You value physical and spiritual health. It appears you have, for the most part, put a plan in place to express these values in your experiences.

Greg: That's true. I never thought of it that way.

Therapist: What else do you value that can be part of your life plan—you know, your "life work"?

Greg: My son. I want to have a better relationship and more contact with my son.

Therapist: Perfect. We can work on the specific actions for this goal in counseling. You see, Greg, these are the things that are meaningful to you and bring you peace and satisfaction. Think of these things as a source of direction for your life.

Greg: Yes, but my previous therapist said that I had to work through my grief issues from my divorce.

Therapist: Greg, constantly attending to what your therapist said three years ago only begets hurtful feelings—it is not what is good for you now. In fact, dwelling on these thoughts and feelings is harmful. It's stealing your life away. Remember: when you dwell on these thoughts you are riding the bus. And in order to live your life, you have to get off the bus.

Greg: Ok, I see your point. So, how can I get this out of my mind? I can't stop thinking about my ex—our problems, the divorce.

Therapist: The first step is to realize that you can be the observer of your thoughts and feelings. Take a step back. See your thoughts as objects. They are not you—they're the bus. You are neither the bus nor the ride, and you can decide not to board. It is important to view these thoughts and feelings as if they are passing by you, rather than defining you.

Greg: That's hard to do. They seem to take me over. They're overwhelming.

Therapist: Yes. If you focus on them, worrying they won't go away, they will engulf you. But if you begin to see them as separate from you, if you become the observer of them, you can really move on and experience what you value in your life. You can focus on something other than your mind. These unproductive thoughts in your mind are the bus, delivering repetitive thoughts and feelings about the grief work you were recommended years ago. When you are able to become more aware of this, you will begin to learn to focus on really living again—living fully in the present in ways consistent with your life plan.

Greg: Okay. So I'm not supposed to think about the past over and over and if I do that then it would be riding the bus. Right?

Therapist: That's right. For you, Greg, reading scriptures every morning brings you peace. When you concentrate on these scriptures, you are off the bus. Another off-the-bus activity you've shared with me is when you are helping others. In these times, you are focused on something other than those negative feelings that stream into your thoughts. When you are helping others, you are off the bus and living your life.

Greg: Oh, I've never heard of this type of thing. I always thought it was good to think.

Therapist: Yes, many people—teachers, parents, and therapists included—believe that thinking and feeling are good things. I take a different perspective. I believe that thinking and feeling, though unavoidable and important at times, are highly overrated. For you, Greg, it's important that you begin to live life in the present. When you do this, you are not riding the bus, focusing on repetitive thoughts and emotions. Engage in the activities and experiences that give you peace and satisfaction—get off the bus!

Greg: Yes, this past couple of weeks I read that book over and over, and I thought a lot about my past. I also stopped reading my morning scriptures. I spent a lot of time alone—thinking, crying.

Therapist: I realize that my bus explanation sounds too simple. However, implementing this method requires awareness, practice—and lots of it. Perfection is not attainable, but incremental progress certainly is.

Greg: Let me go over it again to ensure I have it right. When I am thinking too much about the past and it's making me upset, I'm riding the bus. You want me to get off the bus. This means you want me to focus on some activity that expresses my values in a productive way. You want me to focus on what I want to do, what I value, something that I am doing right at that time, and I can call this my life plan.

Therapist: Yes, Greg, you have it. Again, remember there is no perfection in this. You especially must also get off the perfection bus, which is one you often ride.

Greg: Oh—yeah, that's my obsession, perfectionism. Okay, I can work on that. I can work on staying off that bus, too.

Therapist: Greg, I suggest that you counteract the perfectionism by putting time limits on your activities. When cleaning and organizing, plan to spend only thirty minutes—not hours and hours until you are exhausted and it is done perfectly.

Greg: Okay, you're right. That will be hard, but I can see how doing it that way will help me. Time limits, time limits.

Therapist: I'd like to see you next week to see how you do. See how many times you are able to get off the bus. Use this metaphor to help you remember to engage in your life fully.

Greg: Okay, I have an appointment already scheduled. I'll try to stay off the bus and focus on what I value.

Greg continued in therapy on a regular basis. He began to focus on the things that he valued in his life. He then defined his priorities to focus on every day and every week. From time to time he still became stuck in obsessive thoughts or actions but he would identify them as buses and would use his counseling to help him regain balance and get off the bus. This allowed him to fully engage in the healthy activities that he identified as important in his life plan.

Have you ever experienced an obsession that distracted your attention from the many experiences life offers? In the future, do you think you could use some of the keys we have discussed to get off the bus, freeing yourself from the grips of obsession?

Immoral and Violent Thought Intrusions

In the therapist-client dialogue presented next, Bill is obsessively caught up in heinous thoughts. He wonders why he had the hideous thought of killing his wife, children and committing suicide. The thought just came to him one day out of the blue. The shock of it made it stick in his mind. He couldn't shake it. Questions inundated his mind, he repeatedly asked himself, *Why me? Why did I think this? Why are these thoughts happening? What does it mean?*

Bill, a forty-year account executive, was mild-mannered, shy and quite intellectual. He was a man with high moral standards and a stable upbringing. He expressed the disturbance he felt because of his thoughts, and the fear stirred by the idea of acting out those images that were now scarred in his mind. Bill had no history of self-harm or aggression toward anyone.

We join Bill during one of his therapy sessions.

Bill: I can't stand it anymore! No matter what I do to distract myself from these thoughts, they just keep coming back. I'm scared that if they keep coming back, someday I might act on them. I do not intend to harm anyone, but I think they might lead to that. Even as recent as this week I had thoughts of killing my boss and wife. I'm not even mad at either of them. It's been horrible. I'm scared. Why are these thoughts coming to me?

Therapist: I can see that these thoughts are tremendously disturbing to you. But the history of your conduct—which includes how you've lived your life, your moral upbringing, your moral beliefs about right and wrong—is clearly established. The heinous thoughts that you experience represent the exact opposite of who you are. In fact, that's why these thoughts are so profoundly disturbing to you; they simply do not fit. They don't belong in someone like you.

The second reason these thoughts are hard to let pass is that, by your own description of your personality and characteristics, you are a meticulous perfectionist. You have a graduate degree and you're extremely analytical. Your brain is well developed, and now it appears to be stuck on solving this, a peculiar problem of thinking. You have a very tenacious brain, and now it's in overdrive trying to resolve why you keep thinking these tormenting thoughts.

Bill: These thoughts are scaring me. Why do I have them?

Therapist: To start with, you must realize that the question, "Why do these thoughts come to me?" is part of the problem. Your brain simply won't let go of this question until it's resolved. This is why these thoughts are tormenting you. This type of question defies clear resolution.

Bill: Will I always have these thoughts? I try to distract myself, but it doesn't work. I'm afraid that I will never have any peace. These thoughts keep me awake at night and interrupt me at work. They're constant. I'm frightened I might act on these thoughts one day!

Therapist: I can see how these thoughts are shocking and overwhelming. When these thoughts come to you, they take you over. To reduce these thoughts and their impact, it is important to view them as external. In other words, the thoughts do not reflect who you really are. As you develop an ability to observe these thoughts, you are even an observer of the emotions these thoughts evoke.

The metaphor I use to help clients identify when they get stuck in persistent thought is what I describe as riding the bus. One helpful way to consider such thinking is to visualize riding a bus whenever you experience these thoughts. I often use the metaphor of riding the bus to help clients externalize this type of thinking. This allows clients to step back and become the observer of their thoughts.

When a heinous thought arises with an uneasy feeling, you must recognize that you are on the bus. Riding the bus may even include such self-reflecting questions as, *Why are these thoughts happening to me?; I shouldn't have such thoughts; What do these thoughts mean?; Will I act on these thoughts?; or, This is a terrible and frightening ride.*

Bill: That's exactly what goes on in my head. So what you're saying is that when these thoughts and emotions come, I say to myself, *I'm riding the bus.* Is that right?

Therapist: Exactly. To make you even more prepared and aware, when you notice these thoughts emerging, think of yourself as at the bus stop. This will allow you to actively decide against boarding the bus and, instead, engage in productive activity on which to concentrate. But remember: at the bus stop, you know that another bus will come. So instead of trying to hide from these thoughts, be ready to acknowledge them. Accept them—then let them go. Don't board the bus.

Bill: Okay, I understand what you mean. But I am still not clear about why these thoughts are happening to me.

Therapist: As I said before, this question is part of the problem. Your brain simply won't let go of this question until it's resolved and, unfortunately, this type of question lacks resolution. In other words, there is no sufficient answer. By way of explanation, what I can offer is this: You have a superb mind with tenacious analytical skills, and when these thoughts come, they strike your mind as outlandish and incongruent with whom you really are. The thoughts are at odds with your moral standards evidenced by your behavior, and that's why they disturb you. Your mind's response to this disruption is to solve the problem—so you keep thinking, analyzing, asking why. But these are questions that simply

Get Off the Bus

have no resolution so you must develop the ability to recognize when thinking is in overdrive and becomes a bus ride. The question, "Why?" is at times itself neither healthy nor productive.

Bill: So how do I get rid of these thoughts?

Therapist: First, you must realize that these thoughts are simply just thoughts. When a thought pulls up, say to yourself, *I'm not getting on the bus. I'm not going for the ride.* Next, focus on something external, something other than your thoughts. Many people find it useful to practice focused breathing—that is, slowly and deliberately feeling the temperature of the air entering and leaving your nostrils. Feel the expansion and the contraction of your abdomen upon each breath. Intensely focusing on each breath helps you overcome your cycling thoughts. It helps you get off the bus. You won't be perfect at this at first, but you will notice your concentration and focus improving with each breath.

Bill: So if I just focus on breathing I don't entertain my thoughts?

Therapist: It will be very challenging at first, but you can do it.

Bill: What if I get that sick, nauseated feeling?

Therapist: That, too, is a bus. Focused breathing is especially useful for helping calm your emotional responses. This type of breathing is designed to relax you and reduce your emotional state. When you first try focused breathing, try breathing in on a one-count, hold it four counts, and then breathe out on two counts. Do these ten-to-twenty times. After you've practiced counted breathing, you can just breathe in normal full breaths, focusing on each breath, in and out.

Bill: Breathing seems like it would help for a while—but it seems limited in scope, you know, in terms of getting rid of the thoughts.

Therapist: True. Breathing isn't a total fix. But focused breathing will help you center yourself. You will find calmness between breaths, and this will allow you to reorient your response to these thoughts. You can stay on the bus or you can engage in productive activity in which you find value, activity conducive to the goals comprising your life plan. What can you engage in at home that will occupy your full attention, something that you value?

Bill: I could focus on my kids.

Therapist: Yes, that's a good idea. Raising your children is something you value—and children, of course, can be very engaging. You can intently focus on your children: engage them in discussion, find out what their interests are, focus on what they're communicating, what they are observing, what they are learning. Sometimes while talking with your children use active listening, which entails paraphrasing what your child has spoken to you before responding. This takes real concentration. There are also routine things that you could engage in more intensely, like concentrating on fixing dinner—chopping vegetables, tasting your food, even cleaning up afterwards.

Bill: I see. So the idea is to not allow my mind to wander or dwell on the fact that a heinous thought pulled up at the stop. Don't ride the bus—I think I can do this.

Bill attended counseling sessions weekly for the next three months. Counseling reassured him that he would not act on his heinous thoughts. Over time, Bill developed focused breathing and present focus, both of which served to reduce the frequency of Bill's bus rides.

We can see how Bill became trapped in his own thinking. Recall when the therapist explains:

Therapist: ...the question "Why do these thoughts come to me?" is part of the problem. Your brain simply won't let go of this question until it's resolved. This is why these thoughts are tormenting you. This type of question defies clear resolution.

Continuing later:

Therapist: ...To reduce these thoughts and their impact, it is important to view them as external. In other words, remember: the thoughts do not reflect who you really are. As you develop an ability to observe these thoughts, you are even an observer of the emotions these thoughts evoke.

What activities or people do you truly value in your life? Can you devote more intense present focus to them? Begin to realize the satisfaction that present focus bestows upon what you value most in life.

Identify thought patterns that may qualify as obsessive or repetitive thinking. Try to apply the methods discussed in the therapist-client exchanges to your own life.

Chapter 6

Depression

"The real mission you have in life is to make yourself happy, and in order to be happy, you have to look at what you believe, the way you judge yourself, the way you victimize yourself."

—Don Miguel Ruiz, *The Mastery of Love*

This chapter focuses on clients suffering from symptoms attributed to depression, which are generally described as feeling sad, blue or hopeless. Individuals who are depressed may experience anxiety and lose interest in activities previously enjoyed while others experience mood swings and outbursts of anger. Changes in sleep and appetite patterns, as well as weight fluctuation, are also symptoms attributed to depression. As with anxiety, depression is often associated with obsessive thinking patterns. These thoughts are often characterized by low self-esteem, self-loathing, regret, guilt and even suicidal contemplation. Given the excessively exerted mental activity of cycling thoughts, those suffering from depression generally report depleted physical energy. Depression may spawn negative thinking of one's past, present and future. These thoughts, in turn, further provoke destructive emotional states. These vicious cycles of

Get Off the Bus

negativity can be devastating, affecting one's relationships, work performance, and engagement in life activities.

In the cases presented next, observe how clients suffering from the symptoms of depression benefit from therapy. Note the various ways in which these individuals find the strength to get back into their lives and, applying key steps, get off the bus.

Think about a time in your life you may have experienced a bout of depression. Which keys might have helped you? Could these keys help you curb future periods of depression?

Depression Before and After the Affair

Elly suffered from a depressed mood, which lingered and grew worse. Elly's depression led her to make decisions that caused major marital issues. As you read this therapist-client dialogue, observe the effects of Elly's depression before and after her affair. Consider how her therapy—in helping her identify the origins of her depression—helps her finally apply the keys to overcome it.

We join Elly midsession as she describes the aftermath of her extramarital affair.

Elly: I'm so depressed. I ruined my marriage. I feel so horrible about myself. I don't know how my husband can even stand to be around me anymore.

Therapist: Tell me what happened. I see here that you were discharged from the psychiatric hospital about a week ago, following an incident in which you overdosed on pills. Did you intend to end your life?

Elly: Yes, I don't know if I can live with myself after what I've done. I had an affair, and now when I think about it, I get sick to my stomach.

Therapist: Okay, let's take a look at what was happening before the affair. What were you experiencing? I can see that this has made you sick and we need to look at possible causes.

Elly: What do you mean?

Therapist: Well, how were you doing before the affair? Were you bored? Angry? Sad? Depressed? What was going on inside your mind? What were your emotions? What were your thoughts?

Elly: I was angry and resentful, I guess. My husband was working long hours and I felt all alone. When he came home, I didn't feel like he wanted to be with me. He would watch sports on television or have his guy friends over.

Therapist: What were you doing while your husband was at work? Did you also work?

Elly: Yes, I worked part-time.

Therapist: Do you still have the job?

Elly: No. After I went to the hospital, my husband and I decided it would be better if I stayed home and gave myself some time to heal.

Therapist: How do you feel about this now?

Elly: I feel even guiltier now because I'm not contributing financially.

Therapist: Do you and your husband want to try to work things out and stay married?

Elly: Yes, that's what I want. He says he wants to try and work things out, too.

Therapist: Do you think he would be willing to come in to support you and hear what I have to say?

Elly: Yes, he is very supportive—but he is having such a hard time. And I don't blame him. I can't stand the thought of what I've put him through. I know it must be horrible for him. I'm not sure he can ever get past this and forgive me.

Therapist: That, of course, is his challenge. You have other challenges. I am willing to try to help you both. It will take a bit of work on both your parts.

Elly: I'm willing to do anything if it'll help us.

Therapist: How much time do you spend thinking about what you did or about what your husband might be thinking or experiencing?

Elly: I spend almost every waking moment thinking about how I ruined our lives, how I hurt him so badly. I just wanted to die. I took the pills and the next thing I knew, I was in the hospital. Now I think, "How humiliating, now my whole family knows that I tried to kill myself!" I'm so ashamed.

Therapist: That's quite a load on your back. Would you be willing to work with me to lighten that load some?

Elly: Yes.

Therapist: Okay, is it fair to say that before the affair happened you were unhappy, depressed and even resentful toward your husband?

Elly: Yes.

Therapist: How frequently did you think about how your husband was not paying attention to you or your relationship?

Elly: I thought about it all the time—all day. He would come home and do something like turn on the television without even talking to me first. Then I would snap. We would argue and I would cry. But nothing ever changed.

Therapist: So, back then you spent a lot of time in your head dwelling on thoughts and feelings about how angry and resentful you were toward your husband. And now you grind on feeling guilty about what you have done, what your husband must be going through.

Elly: Yes.

Therapist: When people obsess about thoughts and feelings, I refer to this as riding the bus. It's a shorthand expression I use to help people identify thoughts and feelings as external, which makes them accessible, tangible. Riding the bus, grinding on about thoughts and feelings, is not healthy—it's only further depressing. This pattern of obsessively thinking, by making you sick, robs you of life.

Elly: It really has made me sick—to the point that I did not want to live anymore. So, how do you get off the bus?

Therapist: We will work on exactly that. But first, I need to know a little more about what happened. Then I can help you begin to help yourself. The idea is to manage your thoughts and feelings, rather than allowing thoughts and feelings to manage your every move. How did your affair start?

Elly: An acquaintance from high school started communicating with me on Facebook and one thing led to another.

Therapist: So, in addition to grinding on about anger, resentment, and depressed moods, did you also spend a lot of time fantasizing over your Facebook interactions?

Elly: Yes. I used to look forward to getting online and communicating with him. I thought about getting on Facebook a lot. I thought about him a lot. After a few weeks of daily correspondence, we decided to get together. We met for lunch and ended up in bed. After that, I couldn't stop thinking about what an awful thing I did. I just wanted to die.

Therapist: Getting hooked on the Facebook connection was in many ways a fantasy bus, which you rode to avoid your symptoms of depression, which coincided with the feelings you were experiencing about your husband—also a bus. Again, you went back inside your head, back to the fantasy bus, transferred to the guilt bus, then the husband bus, and back again to the fantasy bus. It seems like your anger and depression made you a frequent—if not constant—bus rider. You were always inside your head. To cope, you boarded the fantasy bus, swinging from one mood to another, until you met your friend. After the affair, you boarded the guilt and shame bus only to find yourself trapped, unable to disembark. At that point, the only exit you saw off the bus was in death. Am I following this so far?

Elly: That pretty much sums it up. Now I live in the mess I created. I am riding one bus or another most of the time.

Therapist: Elly, part of my purpose during our meetings will be to help you learn how to get off the bus. I would like to see you find peace and live your life again. I would also like to meet your husband the next time you come in. I'm sure he's riding a different bus. No doubt, he is suffering with hurt, anger and distrust. These are the buses that he's riding.

Elly: Yeah, now it looks like we both live on the bus. I brought a list of the medications I've been taking. What do you think about these?

Therapist: The medicines you're taking are designed to make the bus rides shorter and less intense. The bedtime medicine is designed to put you to sleep, even if you are on the bus. But like I said, our job in these meetings is to help you get off the bus—or even better, to not board in the first place.

When you are feeling guilt, shame, resentment, you are riding the bus. Thoughts and feelings of anger and resentment, thoughts and feelings of abandonment, thoughts and feelings of boredom and even ostensibly positive distractions, like Facebook fantasies, are all bus rides that you've been taking. All of these take you away from your life. They are not healthy for you.

Now it seems like you're spending most of your day riding the guilt, shame, and humiliation bus. You are dwelling on self-critical thoughts, which leave you to fear the future. These cycling thoughts and feelings are taking your life away. Without positively contributing to your life in any way, these emotional cycles cannot help you resolve your marital problems.

Elly: So, how do I stop thinking?

Therapist: It's impossible to stop thoughts from coming. However, it is possible to stop dwelling on the thoughts. So, when a thought bus pulls up in your head, you need to notice it, accept it, and then resist the temptation to ride. In your current state, you are addicted to riding the bus, which leaves you exhausted and no closer to any resolution or direction. So, once you notice the bus—that is, once the thought or emotion emerges—you need to remind yourself not to board. In a sense, you become an outside observer of those thoughts and emotions by conceptually converting them into a bus. You get a little distance from them. This makes it easier to slow down the repetitive thoughts and emotions.

Elly: How do you keep from getting right back on the bus? I am bombarded with these thoughts. They are constant. They come over and over again.

Therapist: Yes, I know it seems impossible and overwhelming at first. You will need to try a couple of things. First, notice that throughout our discussion today you have become an observer of your own thoughts and emotions. The thoughts and the emotions are not you. They are separate from you. Realizing this is a big first step. Recognizing you are not your thoughts or feelings, but the observer thereof, is huge.

Elly: Okay.

Therapist: Second, when you notice the bus pulling up, tempting you to ride, you must refocus and engage in your life. Focus on what is in front of you—right then, right there, in the present. If you are walking, focus on each step—consider how your muscles feel when you move, what the pavement feels like against your feet. If you are cleaning, focus on the dirt and your cleaning actions—every movement. If you are talking to your husband, intensely focus on his words. Paraphrase back to him in your own words what you have heard.

Elly: I think I can do that.

Therapist: Choose to do healthy activities that keep you off the bus. Activities like playing a musical instrument, working out, practicing focused breathing, meditating and doing yoga—all of these can be helpful. Above all, identify

Get Off the Bus

your values and make the decision to immerse yourself in activities reflecting your values. Focusing intensely and fully concentrating on the present moment is the goal. Present focus is an important skill for you to develop.

Elly continued in therapy weekly for about ten weeks, then once a month for a year. Her husband also participated in many of these sessions. As anticipated, his therapy homework mainly focused on anger, hurt, trust and control issues. He would ride these buses frequently. The rides were intense, especially in the beginning of therapy. After some time, Elly's husband was able to reduce the frequency of his bus rides and he began to understand the conditions his wife experienced that led up to her affair. In time, he was able to forgive her. He began to understand how his wife created her own depression by dwelling on negative thoughts and emotions. He began to understand how her Facebook fantasy and affair were dysfunctional ways of her coping with or escaping from her depression. This understanding allowed him to forgive her—but he was left with major trust issues. He worked very hard in counseling to view his own thoughts and feelings of distrust as bus rides. He became more adept at focusing and interacting with his wife and daughter.

Elly also made progress—but more slowly than her husband. She would not only ride her own buses, occasionally she would ride the 'presuming others' feelings bus,' wondering how awful her husband must feel about her. During a six-month follow up session, both Elly and her husband independently expressed that they were experiencing a more positive relationship with each other, even agreeing they were "much closer now than before the affair."

When have you made poor decisions in a committed relationship? Were your decisions influenced by repetitive thoughts and feelings? Perhaps the more you dwelled, the greener the grass became on the other side of the fence. Keeping repetitive thinking and feeling from dominating your life is an ongoing challenge.

Low Self-Worth After Sexual Trauma

Many people who have lived through severely traumatic events often later report low self-esteem, anxiety, and depression. Those subjected to or witnesses of traumatic events often report difficulty separating the experience of who they are in the present from the traumatic experience of their past. This interferes with their ability to relax, have normal relationships and sleep. Furthermore, it often prevents them from ever feeling at peace. After someone experiences severe trauma—a car accident, a death, a violent act, among many other tragedies—the associated thoughts and feelings can become so salient that they become confused with experience of the present.

Have you experienced a traumatic experience? The tragic death of someone, an accident, an act of violence? Sometimes overwhelming thoughts and feelings start right away and other times they catch up to us after a delay—in some cases, even after years have passed. You may wonder if you will ever feel normal again.

In the next therapist-client dialogue presented, we meet Emily, a 32-year-old bookkeeper, who came to counseling to address the debilitating effects of her depression. Her symptoms included low self-esteem, suicidal thinking that once culminated in a suicide attempt and immense sexual anxiety. Traumatic experiences in Emily's life, the memories of which cycled in subsequent feelings and thoughts, haunted her. She had not been able to separate herself—the woman she became, who she was in the present—from the origins of her trauma.

We join Emily during her first session of counseling, after she and the therapist have been introduced to one another.

Therapist: When you thought about coming to see me, what did you want to accomplish?

Emily: Well, I'm not sure. I guess I just wanted to vent. I feel lonely, depressed, and I'm anxious about socializing or dating. I want to date—yet I feel burned out on dating.

Therapist: Have you thought of anything in your history that might cause this type of anxiety?

Emily: Yes. Please forgive me for crying, I—I just have trouble with—I—oh, I'm so sorry, this is just so difficult for me to say out loud. I was raped. I was a senior in high school. I was out on a first date with a boy and he raped me at knifepoint. No one found out about this except the boy who did this to me. Because of what happened, I feel no one would want me. But, really, the guys who date me don't even know what happened. Like recently, I dated this guy—and I thought things were going pretty well—but then out of nowhere he never calls me again. I mean, how can men be so cruel and inconsiderate? So now, I shy away from dating anyone. I even get nervous meeting anyone new.

Therapist: I can see that what happened to you hurt you deeply and these events are the cause of much pain and many of your issues. I believe I can help you. It will take a bit of work on your part but I think you can do it. May I ask you a few questions that do not directly relate to the major concerns that you have brought up?

The therapist provides the client with words of comfort, empathy and reassurance. Whether it is from a friend or a therapist, this support is an essential element in supporting someone and facilitating progress. It is the core of social support and a therapeutic alliance.

Emily: Sure, I'm sorry. I just unloaded. I am just so overwhelmed.

Therapist: No worries, I just don't want to overwhelm you even more. So, first off, do you work or are you a student?

Emily: I work.

Therapist: Where?

Emily: A financial firm.

Therapist: How long have you worked there?

Emily: Five years.

Therapist: Well, that's impressive. It sounds like you are a good worker; after five years you must be respected and feel accepted at work.

Emily: Yes, I am. I don't make enough money to pay my bills though. I'm struggling financially, and I'm depressed and miserable about my debt. I made some bad financial decisions. I worry about money all the time.

Therapist: So, in addition to the trauma issues, you are also under a great deal of stress related to your finances and debt.

Emily: Yes, I am sad and worried most of the time. Then I get lonely and depressed. I start remembering what happened to me. I blame myself. Yet I know there is no way I could have known what those guys intended to do to me.

Therapist: So, you spend a lot of time putting yourself down?

Emily: Yeah, I feel like I'm damaged goods. I ask myself, *Why me?* I think I somehow caused what happened or think I must have deserved it. At the same time, I'm angry and resentful that it happened to me.

Therapist: You know, Emily, you are beating yourself up over and over again. That's something we're going to need to address here in counseling. One of the goals of your counseling will be to help you stop beating yourself up about what happened to you in the past. We're going to work on enabling you to leave the past behind—to stop dwelling on it and the feelings associated with it.

Emily: That would be nice. Sorry I'm using up all your tissues here.

Therapist: Let's take a look at the fact that you—like just about everyone else—reflect and make judgments about yourself. This ability actually creates problems. This can lead to overwhelming, repetitive thoughts and emotions, which are uniquely human—and unfortunately, uniquely unproductive. Though your experiences are in the past, these cycling thoughts keep animating your mind, keep digging them up, preventing your progress. I would like your counseling to help you separate yourself—who you are today, I mean, including all the potential your future holds—from your past trauma.

Emily. I need that for sure.

Therapist: Let me explain how sometimes our minds overthink things and work against us. Animals tend not to get post-traumatic stress disorder. They are not self-critical. We can learn from animals how to live more in the present and avoid mentally unhealthy thinking and emotions. For example, if a cat were pushed out of a tree by another cat, would the cat think, "I'm not worthy of climbing trees. I should not hang out with other cats when I'm in trees. I must have deserved being pushed out of the tree. What's wrong with me? Other cats don't like me; I don't want to hang out with other cats because they don't want to hang out with me. I am a clumsy cat and I shouldn't have fallen out of the tree. I'm afraid that if I go up the tree, I will be rejected by the other cats and will fall again. I'm scared to climb up trees now. I'm dumb because I got pushed out of the tree. Nobody will respect me because I didn't have good balance and got pushed out of the tree."

Just imagine if a cat entertained such thinking. It would experience overwhelming emotions. These emotions would probably prevent the cat from playing with the other cats or climbing up into trees ever again. The feelings that the cat might experience might include loneliness, fear, panic, depression, anxiety, anger, resentment, and so on. Yet when we talk about a cat having this experience we find it preposterous. When this type of thinking happens to people, however, we view it as "normal"!

I call this pattern of thinking and feeling riding the bus. Riding the bus is a metaphor, of course—but it actually helps us identify problems of thought by assigning recognizable labels to them. It is an expression I use to describe when your brain focuses too much on what your mind is delivering. This type of thinking and emoting—what I call riding the bus—can be very unhealthy and disruptive to a person's life. So, the goal in many of my counseling sessions is to help people get off the bus.

Emily: Yeah, I think I understand. Sometimes I feel like I'm living at the bus terminal.

Therapist: Getting back to the cats, we find it incomprehensible to view a cat riding the bus—thinking, feeling, or acting this way—and yet, people are on the bus all the time. Such thinking is not healthy. These bus rides rob you of your life.

Emily: So how do I not be that especially self-conscious cat riding the bus?

Therapist: I like your sense of humor. When we allow ourselves to spin with repetitive thoughts we are riding the bus. It sounds to me like you're riding the bus most of the time. In our work together, I am confident you will learn not to get on the bus. It may take some time, but you can do it.

Just outside my office window, there is a bus stop. A bus pulls up every five to ten minutes. I typically notice the bus when it pulls up, but then I focus on something else. I don't rush out and jump on the bus just because the bus stops and opens its doors. I stay here focused with you—I am present.

From what you tell me, you are stuck dwelling on negative judgments about yourself. For you, one of the buses might be called the damaged-goods bus or the nobody-wants-me bus. What you've experienced, being raped, is absolutely horrible. You are very brave to be here addressing this traumatic event and the effect it has had on you. The ongoing tragedy, however, is that your own cycling thoughts and emotions accomplish only more damage. Your thoughts and feelings, while generated from physically and emotionally traumatic events, are presently precluding your happiness. Our work together will address altering your attention away from those thinking and emotional patterns. You will learn how to get off the bus and into your life.

Emily: Ok, well—but when I try to start thinking about getting out and meeting guys, I start feeling overwhelmed and anxious. Then I think that no one will want to be with me anyway. Then I get depressed, and so overwhelmed.

Therapist: That must be demoralizing.

Emily: Two weeks ago, my sister took me to the hospital after I overdosed on sleep and depression medications. I couldn't stand it anymore. I wanted to die. I was scared to leave the house and socialize. But staying housebound—isolated and withdrawn—put me into a deep depression. I thought about myself as worthless, never having any hope. I wanted to die.

Therapist: Emily, you come across to me as a bright and attractive young woman. You have a good sense of humor. You demonstrate these characteristics every day at your work. In your personal life and in your mind, however, you are definitely riding the bus.

Emily: So how do I get off the bus? It seems overwhelming. How can anybody stop thinking?

Therapist: First, to stop thinking is not possible. Such a goal, I believe, would set you up to fail. Thoughts will come and thoughts will go. When the thought bus pulls up, you need to be aware of it as a bus—and you don't need to board. Getting a little separation between you and the bus can be helpful. You may begin to realize that you can become the observer of your thoughts and feelings, not part of them.

Begin to notice when the bus stops in your mind that the choice is yours to ride or not. Sometimes you will discover that you've accidentally been on the bus for a while. In these times, you can then decide that you want to get off the bus. To do this, you'll need to concentrate one hundred percent on something productive—as simple as your breathing, as complex as playing a musical instrument. Whatever it is, concentrate. Your brain needs to focus on something other than what your mind is delivering. The idea is that to get off the bus, you have to engage activities in which you find value. To accomplish this, most people need to develop it over time. Emily, have you ever had any hobbies—played a sport, a musical instrument, pursued an interest in art, perhaps?

Emily: I used to play trumpet in the university marching band.

Therapist: Perfect. When you were performing and playing the notes during a performance, were you—as I say—on the bus, worrying about something, feeling guilty, or inadequate?

Emily: No, I thoroughly enjoyed playing. Sometimes before we performed, I could get very nervous and worry that I would play the notes off key and be noticed. But once the performance began, I was completely off the bus.

Therapist: Ok, so what do you think I would say about what you were doing before those performances?

Emily: You would probably say that I was riding the bus before performances.

Therapist: Exactly.

Emily left her session with a new sense of purpose, equipped with the keys to pursue life in the present and the metaphors to find her way off the bus. What follows came several sessions later.

Emily: I'm doing so much better now.

Therapist: Tell me more. What's happening, Emily? Are you staying off the bus?

Emily: The other day I went to a football game with a group of people. I had fun, but during the game several of the people who knew each other better than they knew me were talking about going to a party at someone's house after the game. I began to notice that no one specifically invited me. I began to assume they didn't like me. I began to think that they didn't want me to attend the party. But I became aware this time that I might be riding the bus. To stay off, I focused only on getting to the party. After the game, I went home. I immediately focused on changing my clothes and getting a cab to the party. I had a great time. The people there were actually really glad to see me. We talked and laughed until three in the morning.

Get Off the Bus

Therapist: What else, Emily?

Emily: Well, you know I've been miserable because of my finances. I learned that the two loans I took out to preserve my apartment lease were charging something like six hundred percent interest. I thought about declaring bankruptcy. At first, I thought this was an impossible bus for me to get off of—but I switched my focus from the endless-financial-gloom-and-doom bus ride to proactively solving my financial nightmare. I called a bankruptcy attorney. I called for advice and the first visit was free. He advised against bankruptcy. The attorney called the check-cashing store. The attorney explained to the cash store that they had exorbitantly profited on the interest already paid on my account. The attorney negotiated a payback with an annual interest rate of six percent, rather than the six hundred percent! Now the payback is affordable and it allows me to live well and still get out of debt.

So, instead of living the bus, I got off of it! I dealt with the situation and implemented a plan and stayed off the bus. I can see how this getting off the bus thing really works.

Therapist: That's great, Emily. Instead of dwelling on financial doom and gloom, you saw it as a problem to be solved, putting a plan in place. Then you focused on the plan while putting it into effect. Perfect.

Emily: I've also been dealing better with my emotions concerning my experience of sexual abuse. When I have a thought about what happened to me, I say to myself, *It's the bus,* and I don't get on for the ride. I find something else to do. I will call a friend. I also took up guitar, so I frequently practice that. I don't ride the bus. I let it pass by without me. I still have my rough moments. At times, it's hard not to ride—but eventually, I'm able to get off the bus. And a lot sooner than I used to.

Therapist: Emily, this is so great! More and more, you will improve on leaving this terrible trauma behind you—and, in the process, you will separate your life from it.

Emily: Dating is still a problem for me. I think about how I've been dumped by guys in the past. I think about what they might be thinking. How they are judging me. Now I tend to avoid conversations with men. It's difficult for me to focus on small conversational talk when I'm already on the I'm-going-to-get-dumped-anyway bus.

Emily continued in weekly treatment for about three months. She became skilled at catching herself on the bus as she developed the ability to get off the bus with precision. As she progressed, she learned to not even board the bus in the first place.

Emily developed a healthy social life, attending as many events and activities as her work schedule would allow. Each time she planned to join her friends it was a challenge for her not to ride the bus, as she could easily stay home and avoid social contact. However, she persistently stayed focused on the next step to put herself in the mix of life.

Several months later, Emily returned for additional counseling appointments. She explained that she knew she was riding the bus again. She reported that she had called in sick to work, shutting herself in her apartment for a few days. She admitted that she mentally pounded herself with her thoughts that she again began thinking of herself as "damaged goods," "not worthy," and that she "will never find a good guy." She shared that she had been dating a really nice guy and things were going great until he unexpectedly broke things off. He told her he wasn't emotionally ready to continue in the relationship as he still had thoughts about his last relationship.

Emily sobbed. She was hurt and angry. She described her heartbreak. She had finally met a nice young man who treated her well, whom she trusted. They dated for a couple of months, and then it was over! Emily reported a recurrence of thoughts and feelings associated with her rape. She wanted to withdraw from the world.

Emily's continued therapy focused on the intensity of her heartbreak, hurt, and anger, as well as how the intensity was attached to past trauma experienced. Emily began to recognize this. The therapist also told her that breaking up is supposed to hurt and that it may take a while for these feelings to pass. For a while, it might even be necessary for her to ride the heartbreak bus, while being careful not to transfer to the trauma bus. Emily found the strength to take on her challenges. The counseling sessions helped her get through her heartbreak and helped her to re-engage in her life.

Overcoming traumatic experiences in life can be a tremendous challenge. However, if you understand how your emotions and thoughts are operating, you can begin to separate your past from present. Becoming the observer and developing present focus in your life can lead back to living your life. What traumatic experiences do you frequently find yourself thinking about? How can the keys discussed be utilized to overcome these events from your past?

Marital Conflict Leading to Depression

In the therapist-client dialogue presented below, readers are introduced to James. For the most part mentally healthy, James was 52-year-old with a successful career. However, James was experiencing migraines along with other symptoms of depression. His symptoms resulted from ruminations about his frustration with his wife, whom he described as mentally unstable.

We join James at the beginning of his first session.

Therapist: What brings you in today?

James: Well, I'm not sure. I'm not sure if this will help. I am depressed most of the time. I don't have much energy during the day. I plod through my work. I am a highly skilled software developer. My job requires intense concentration. I don't seem to be able to concentrate as well as I used to. I dread going home at night. My wife has a serious mental illness and, as a result, she constantly berates me. I am continually angry with my wife. Recently, I am experiencing more migraine headaches than ever before. I am totally stressed out.

Therapist: It sounds like you have thought through your concerns. This gives me a good start in terms of knowing what pain you are experiencing and what seems to be causing it. When was the last time you recall not being so depressed or angry, not feeling so down? When was the last time that you felt that things were pretty much ok, a time when life was going fairly smoothly?

James: It's been a while. I'd say about three years ago.

Therapist: At that time, three years ago, what types of things were you doing?

James: Well, I was doing many things. I played the piano, I biked long distances with some buddies of mine. I even attended a class on transcendental meditation.

Therapist: That's impressive. Back then, you participated in several activities that allowed you to unplug from the stress. These activities helped you unplug from the worries and irritating thoughts delivered by your mind. What occupies your thoughts now?

James: I constantly think about my wife. I wish she would be calmer. I wish she didn't yell at me. We argue all the time. She berates me. She criticizes everything I do.

Therapist: Do you have friends?

James: Me or us?

Therapist: Well, either.

James: No, she does not have any friends. She talks to our kids on the phone occasionally. She plays games on the Internet most of the time. That's it. I used to have a couple of buddies that I cycled with on the weekends, but I haven't done that in a couple of years.

Therapist: Describe the thought patterns that you now experience.

Get Off the Bus

James: What do you mean?

Therapist: What do you think about, and when? What, as you said, do you think about?

James: When I try to go to sleep my thoughts won't stop. I'm angry with my wife. I wish she could change. I am disappointed in myself. I worry I don't have the energy to do my job. I anticipate and worry about suffering from my next migraine. This keeps me awake at night and distracts me from working during the day. If I could get my wife some help, then things might be better. But she refuses to do anything.

Therapist: This pattern of depressed, angry, and stressful thinking is what I refer to as riding the bus. The goal of our work here will be to help you get off the bus as much as possible.

James: Well, I'm all ears. How do I stay off the bus?

Therapist: Well, James, you—more so than many of my other clients—have some distinct advantages. These advantages will help you overcome the current stress, depression and anger that you're suffering. First, you are very bright. Second, you experienced a time in your life when you effectively managed your thoughts and emotions. These were times when you were able to unplug from thinking, times when you were able to stop riding the bus. You were cycling with friends. You were playing the piano. You were participating in transcendental meditation. You were engaged in living. You got away from riding the bus.

Now it appears that you are riding the bus, thinking about things that are out of your control, wishing that your wife's personality would change. As you have described, when you are the most irritated with her, you seem to antagonize her even further by either withdrawing or arguing. She gets worse instead of better.

James: What are you supposed to do when you are constantly the target of verbal abuse?

Therapist: It seems like you frequently wish that your wife would change. You wish she would not treat you this way. You feel you should not be subjected to her behavior. It seems you take what she says to heart, allowing it to undermine your judgment about yourself. You allow this to happen even though you know she has psychological issues. When you think in this pattern, it's riding the bus for sure. So, taking it personally when she yells at you is riding the bus.

James: Yeah, I can see I'm doing myself damage.

Therapist: You may have noticed that obsessive thinking and rumination are addictive. It's hard to resist. It captivates you. Then it slams you down, leaving you exhausted. It appears that you have become addicted to this pattern of thinking.

Like any addiction, you must be aware of it to face it head on, or it will take you down by surprise. In other words, you must remember that you are living, for now anyway, at the bus stop. You must notice the bus pulling up and consciously decide against getting on. Sometimes you will realize you have already been riding the bus for quite some time. Again, you must get off of it. Riding the bus—dwelling on these thoughts—is exhausting, depressing, and stressful. As you've said, when you dwell on it, it interrupts your sleep, causes migraines and is now interfering with your work.

So, when you see the bus pull up, notice it. Notice it as something separate from you. Next, focus on something in front of you, just like you did when you practiced meditation. Focus on your steps, your breathing.

James: So this method can work like meditation?

Therapist: Yes, concentrate on something that is present, like playing the piano or cycling. These are great ways to focus your mind, which gets you back into living life. Fully concentrating on what you do. Focusing on what is present rather than the unproductive thoughts racing through your mind. Being present and concentrating on the present is the challenge.

James: I like this. I probably should have thought of it myself.

Therapist: What you are doing at any moment is an important point of focus. For example, when you are eating, it is important that you experience your sensations more fully. In the past, you were likely riding the bus—thinking about how awful your wife was making you feel—instead of tasting and enjoying your food. In a sense, the bus ride takes away from your life, takes you away from living. When you are on the bus, you don't notice the temperature of the food, the different textures, the different tastes, or anything. I'm suggesting that you deliberately begin to notice such things. This will help you to stay off the bus and in the present.

James attended approximately ten sessions of therapy. During each session, the therapist illustrated how James was riding the bus with his thoughts and feelings and what he could do to get off the bus. James used the sessions to motivate himself to focus on the present and on what he could control. Later he started to participate in life again. He used the counseling as a supportive checkpoint to maintain his progress. In a short while, James re-engaged in stress-buffering hobbies and became reacquainted with his cycling buddies. His headaches diminished and he began to enjoy life again in spite of his wife's rants.

The therapy dialogue demonstrates how James was able to regain a healthy focus while accepting his wife's pattern of instability. The use of the riding the bus analogy significantly reduced James' cyclical thoughts, which fueled his depression and distress. In addition, James recognized that dwelling on his angry thoughts had caused him to drop the activities that brought him satisfaction and peace in his life.

Instead of getting caught up in his wife's emotional instability, James would listen to his wife with greater concentration, paraphrasing her words back to her. He would be certain that he understood and showed her that he understood. All the while, he avoided any defensive replies. He resisted jumping on the bus and no longer tried to defend himself, constantly arguing with his wife. James reported that he felt much more at peace and, as a result of this, his wife actually reduced the frequency and intensity of her verbal assaults on him. James was able to, for the most part, stay off the bus. As well, he was able again to focus at work.

Do you allow irritation or frustration with a person— someone who you know will not change—to affect your experience? Have you in the past? Did you attempt to talk them into changing or, worse, try to force them to change? These attempts generally only worsen relationships. Consider the fact that your focus on your thoughts caused you to suffer—often times more so than the events from which your thoughts originated. While the person's behavior was transient, subsequent thoughts may have flooded your mind for hours. Focus on something else fully. Make a plan.

Marital Conflict and Divorce Leading to Depression and Anger

Sometimes an individual's depression manifests in outbursts of anger. Instead of blue moods from dwelling on sad thoughts, these people focus on what angers them. This typically does very little to resolve the depression which gives rise to the anger in the first place. Among other things, this can lead to health problems associated with coronary artery disease. Such was the case with Sam. Sam was angry with his soon-to-be ex-wife and his attorney.

We join Sam during his third session of counseling.

Therapist: Hi Sam. How was your week? Anything happen that you want to focus on today?

Sam: No. It was a typical week.

Therapist: All right then. Good to see you today. What do you want to accomplish during our meeting today?

Sam: I'd like to not be so pissed off all the time.

Therapist: That's a good goal, especially good because it helps with your heart problems as well. Anger constricts those arteries.

Sam: Yeah, sometimes I feel like I'm going to burst.

Therapist: Do you get angry in the spur of the moment or burn slowly and heat up?

Sam: I think I do both.

Therapist: Which is more common? Think about it for a moment.

Sam: Well, I spend most of my time thinking about the things that get me upset.

Therapist: Ok, Sam, I consider this type of thinking a bus ride. You're riding the slow-burning-anger bus, which culminates in your outbursts of anger. Think of this expression when you are thinking these thoughts, getting emotionally worked up.

Sam: Yeah, it sounds like I'm riding this bus almost every day.

Therapist: What are they like? What's going through you?

Sam: Well, I'm pissed off that my lawyer isn't finalizing my divorce. I'm ticked off at Mary, my soon-to-be ex-wife. She's now claiming that she can't work full time and she will no doubt be awarded alimony. I mean, give me a break—she's the one who had the affair. Paying alimony bugs the hell out of me.

Therapist: Yup. Those are certainly buses, Sam. You've got to get off the bus by focusing on your plan and your new life.

Sam: Yeah—but this stuff just isn't right.

Therapist: Does dwelling on it fix it?

Sam: You have a point there.

Therapist: When you catch yourself drifting into these angry thoughts, don't ride that bus. See them as intruders, enemies attempting to steal your life away.

Sam: So what plan? I can't plan anything until the divorce is final.

Therapist: That's a bus, too.

Sam: Is everything a bus?

Therapist: You've got several going.

Sam: So what can I plan?

Therapist: First, create a plan to communicate with your attorney so he gets your work done.

Sam: Yeah, I should just go sit in his office on a day he's not in court.

Therapist: Sure. If that's what it takes, go for it. However, once you make the plan, watch out for the lawyer bus to come back around. When it does, notice it as the enemy stealing your life. This represents the first step of your plan in place to deal with it. Next, get focused on what you are doing—whether it's visiting your family or tinkering on a project in your garage.

Sam: Ok, I can work on this—but alimony and she can't work full time?

Therapist: Does riding that bus help you live your life, or solve the injustice of the situation?

Sam: No.

Therapist: Well?

Sam: You're right.

Therapist: Sam, you're a good man. You've gone through a couple of really traumatic experiences between bypass surgery and your wife's affair. Those are horrific, gut wrenching—but living on the anger bus is a lot less than you deserve.

Sam: I just keep thinking about this stuff.

Therapist: It's like a drug addiction. You must become more aware of it before you can attend to it. Once you've identified it, have a plan.

Sam: You're right. But I'm worried I will be lonely. I was married for twenty years.

Therapist: So what would I say about that?

Sam: I'm riding another bus.

Therapist: Exactly.

Sam: But it's reality.

Therapist: No, it is not.

Sam: How so?

Therapist: Reality is what your plan is. If you are lonely, you need to plan social opportunities for yourself. At first, it will be uncomfortable to do this—but the eventual outcome will be new friends, reducing loneliness, and maybe even finding a partner.

Sam: I've got some work to do.

Therapist: You can do it. What can you do to remind yourself about riding the bus so that you will be quick to get off of it, or not get on in the first place?

Sam: I'm going to take a photo of the city bus outside this office and use it as a screen saver on my cell phone.

Therapist: Perfect. That's a great idea. When do you want to come back to check in with me?

Sam made good progress then he would lapse into weeks full of anger. Later on in counseling he complained about being worked up and angry with his office manager who he claimed was not performing to his expectations. What follows came a few sessions later when he was discussing this new source of anger.

Sam: Oh, I'm on one today!

Therapist: What's up?

Sam: Well, my office manager isn't doing her job. She shows up late and leaves early. Then I find out that instead of having a voice-to-voice with our product shippers, she has been relying on single sent emails. The product shippers often ignore the emails, resulting in late shipments and orders that aren't sent at all. I'm losing customers because of this and I'm about to blow up.

Therapist: How long has she been coming in late and leaving early?

Sam: I don't know—a long time, over a year.

Therapist: Why don't you write her up?

Sam: Well, I don't want to lose her. I think I'm so angry that I might make her mad and she may just up and quit.

Therapist: Sounds like your own anger scares you out of expressing your thoughts and feelings.

Sam: Well, yeah. I get all worked up about it. My doctor told me to avoid stress. I've had bypass surgery, but this kind of stuff stresses me out to the max. I feel my arteries clogging up!

Therapist: How often do you think about this?

Sam: I think about it off-and-on every day, almost all day long, especially when I'm driving or when I'm alone at home.

Therapist: So, off-and-on all day long you're thinking about how your employee angers you?

Sam: Yeah.

Therapist: So, a person you have hired to solve work problems for you is creating a situation that interferes with your peace of mind throughout the day, seven days a week?

Get Off the Bus

Sam: I never thought of it that way, but yeah. That's about it. The same stuff happened in my marriage until I just blew up and moved out three months ago.

Therapist: Let's examine the role that anger plays in your life. I suspect we may discover it rules you. When someone is angry and they are not productively engaged in something, their anger tends only to increase. In your case, the anger bus is the one you ride most of the time.

Sam: Yep, that's me. I'm riding that bus constantly.

Therapist: To get off the bus, Sam, you will have to consider doing several things.

Sam: I'm all ears. This stuff is killing me.

Therapist: First, you have to take some sort of action with your employee. Write her up for being late. Tell her if she is late again, she will receive a final warning and be terminated the next time she's late. Then you follow the plan.

Sam: Yeah, but I don't want to lose her. I'll be in a real pickle if she's out the door.

Therapist: Sam, that's another bus, a different bus, that's a worry bus.

Sam: Yeah, but it's true.

Therapist: I'm sure it seems that way. However, are you telling me that someone else could not be trained for that job?

Sam: No. I could find someone and train him or her—but it would take a while.

Therapist: It's possible though.

Sam: Of course.

Therapist: Well, it's also possible she may improve if she knows her job is on the line. Right?

Sam: Yeah, it's possible. She makes more money on this job than she would get anywhere else.

Therapist: The goal here, Sam, is to get you off the bus so you can enjoy your time off or get focused on the work you need to do.

Sam: That would be nice.

Therapist: First, you have to realize that you are, in a sense, addicted to your own anger. You're addicted to the anger bus. To stop the addiction you need to increase your awareness of when the bus is coming.

Sam: If I'm aware of it, how will that help?

Therapist: Once you are aware of your anger as a bus, it becomes something external to you. Then you can deal with it. When this bus pulls up, remember that you have a plan in place to remedy the situation. Don't get on the bus just because you're accustomed to it. Instead, engage in something else with your full attention and focus, like doing a hobby or helping a friend. This type of concerted engagement keeps you off the bus.

Sam continued in counseling for the next six months, during which time his divorce process and his work challenges continued. He continued having trouble getting off the anger bus. Later counseling sessions returned to the addictive quality of Sam's bus rides, focusing on ways he could address and overcome his patterned behavior.

Counseling sessions highlighted a shift in Sam's values toward actively living his life in the present. This created a greater awareness and a sense of urgency in Sam. The idea of fully living life motivated him to employ what he had learned in counseling. Specifically, Sam, who had been close to death a year earlier, recognized that his focus on money was not truly meaningful to him anymore.

Due to his near death experience, spending time with his grandchildren, having adventurous trips and staying healthy became his priorities. Counseling helped Sam keep his focus on his life priorities, while enabling him to notice when the anger buses were luring him away from what he truly valued.

By the sixth or seventh month of sessions scheduled once or twice a month, Sam was able to deal with previously provocative situations with a smile, calmness, and peace of mind that allowed him to resolve problems more quickly. He was able to bounce back from unexpected outcomes in life without rage or depression.

Loneliness and Worry Leading to Depression

The combined effects of loneliness with thoughts of worry and hopelessness can engender serious states of depression. Such repetitive thinking leads one to further isolation, which secures only more time in which to think negative thoughts about the future, leading to more serious depression, fatigue, sleep issues, among other problems.

In this next case, Ruth has been suffering from depression for over a year. She is confused, tearful, fatigued, and has lost interest in all of her usual life activities at home, work, and in her social life. What's significant about Ruth's example is the fact that she suffered from her depression for such a long time without seeking any treatment.

We join Ruth during her first sessions of counseling.

Therapist: What brings you in today?

Ruth: I don't want to live. Don't worry, I'm not going to kill myself—but I don't want to live like this either. I'm stressed out and depressed all the time.

Therapist: How long have you felt this depressed?

Ruth: Over a year, but the last three months have been much worse.

Therapist: Is there a situation that is causing you to be more depressed now?

Ruth: Yeah. I'm married, but my husband works in another state. I'm lonely a lot of the time. Our finances are stretched. I don't see how we will work ourselves out of this. I worry about my husband's safety. He works on high-rise construction projects. I worry about him all of the time. I worry that he will be killed on the job. It's dangerous work.

Therapist: Is there anything else going on?

Ruth: Yeah. Several months ago I voluntarily transferred to a new job in a different department. I hate it. I feel like I am constantly under attack.

Therapist: So, you've been depressed for over a year. You're financially strained. You're lonely because you are apart from your husband. You worry about his safety because he works out of state on high-rise construction projects and you hate your new job. That's quite a load. What feelings and thoughts go through your mind when you are experiencing your deepest depression and despair?

Ruth: I'm sorry. Do you have tissues? Sometimes I can't help but let it all out.

Therapist: You're fine.

Ruth: Like I said, I constantly worry about my husband being injured or killed. I keep regretting the fact that I switched jobs. Now I'm stuck. I work at a call center and I take on customer complaints all day long. The customers are mean. They yell, swear, and call me names. I can't stand it.

Therapist: That kind of verbal abuse is tough to take for sure. Are you able to sleep?

Ruth: I haven't slept a full night in over six months. When I get up in the morning, I'm always dragging.

Therapist: Do you have trouble falling asleep or staying asleep?

Get Off the Bus

Ruth: Both. When I'm in bed my mind races with worry. I feel so depressed and lonely.

Therapist: How long does it take you to fall asleep?

Ruth: Sometimes an hour—most of the time, though, it takes at least two hours. I turn on the TV. Sometimes this helps.

Therapist: Do you take any medication?

Ruth: I meet with my medical doctor in a few days to see about medication. So no medications yet.

Therapist: The next time we meet, I will be interested to see what the doctor prescribes.

Ruth: Is there anything I can do? I hate the way I am living now.

Therapist: Right now, when I hear you and observe how down you are, I am reluctant to suggest too much too soon. You appear to be extremely depressed, fatigued, and without energy. I do not want to overwhelm you, so I would like to start slowly. Have you ever participated in anything like yoga or meditation?

Ruth: No.

Therapist: Well the assignment I'd like you to try has to do with your breathing. I call it focused breathing, and it's been shown to have both psychological and physical benefits. Yoga and meditation both are exercises that use focused breathing. But you can do focused breathing without a class, too.

Ruth: How does it work?

Therapist: Well, let's first consider it in a context that would be useful for you. Use focused breathing to help with relaxing just before you fall asleep, for instance.

Ruth: Ok.

Therapist: To do this, you would turn the TV off and get into bed in a comfortable sleeping position.

Ruth: No TV and no music?

Therapist: That's right. Now, watch me breathe while I instruct you. I'll show you. I focus on the air going into my nostrils, sensing the temperature of the air. Concentrating on the air, the cold molecules entering the nostrils, expanding my chest and abdomen, then the warm air exiting my nostrils. Then again. And again.

It's a challenge for me to focus only on my breathing; but when I do, I am not thinking or feeling, I am just focused on the breath. This relaxes me physically and gets me out of thinking.

Ruth: I see. So the trick is to really focus on each breath?

Therapist: Exactly. Focusing on each breath takes you out of your head and away from your worries and negative emotions.

Ruth: Should I just do this breathing in bed?

Therapist: Well, you may want to practice this breathing frequently throughout the day. However, when you want to go to sleep at night, I would like you to turn the TV off and practice focused breathing in bed. I am sure this will help you get to sleep.

Ruth: Okay, I can try this. When should I reschedule with you?

Therapist: I would like you to come in next week after your medical doctor's appointment.

Ruth: Okay, I will schedule something for next Thursday.

Therapist: The focused breathing is a first step and a building block for what follows. I know you have suffered with this depression for a long time, but I want you to know that help is on the way. Next week, we can begin to address the thoughts, emotions and situations that are keeping you down. Good luck with your breathing homework.

When you are suffering emotionally and experiencing depression, it is common to think a visit to the therapist or doctor will make it all better—a quick fix solution. Your friends, your therapist, your doctor, are pulled by your distress to want to "save the day" and may be tempted to tell you "just do this" or "just take that" and "things will be better."

When this happens you may be setting up for a deeper depression and disappointment because when the suggestion or pill does not work, you may become even more hopeless and further entrenched on the bus.

Starting small for a person suffering with depression may mean getting up in the morning and taking a shower—that is it. In Ruth's case, the focused breathing was a small step, but not one held out to build up false hope.

In her next session, Ruth discussed her homework. She talked about how she applied focused breathing to become less stressed and more relaxed. The therapist then introduced the concept of becoming the observer of her emotions and thoughts. To accomplish this, the therapist uses the riding the bus analogy. The bus analogy is woven into the session to help Ruth regulate her attention and focus on healthy activities. She is encouraged to develop her present focus, as opposed to concentrating on the depressing and demoralizing thoughts that float in and out of her mind.

Therapist: Hi Ruth, before we start up where we left off last week, have there been any major occurrences in your life? Anything that came up that you want to focus on first?

Ruth: No, it's been a typical week.

Therapist: You look like you are doing a little better today. Have you been using the breathing technique we discussed in the last session?

Ruth: Yeah, I've been doing the focused breathing at work and at home before going to sleep.

Therapist: That's so great. Have you been trying to use your breathing to unplug your mind from stress and worry to relax your body? Research shows that this type of breathing is a very helpful exercise with both anxiety and depression.

Ruth: The breathing has helped me to fall asleep almost every night without having the TV on. I do the breathing. I did have one bad night though.

Therapist: Tell me what happened.

Ruth: I got a call from my cousin just before bedtime. She went on and on about her new baby. After I hung up, I lost it. I couldn't sleep. I cried and cried. I thought about the personal infertility I've been dealing with for the past two years. *Why me?* I kept thinking.

Therapist: I'm sorry. It seems your cousin inadvertently triggered a tsunami of emotion within you.

Ruth: Yeah. I went to work the next day in a daze. I was moody and my boss confronted me on the quantity of work I was producing. He said he would need to write me up if the shortfalls continued.

Therapist: Wow. That's a lot of grief and pressure to be under. Today, you seem to have come out of it a bit though. Is that right?

Ruth: Yes, I feel a lot better today.

Therapist: Good. As promised, our work today will focus on your emotions and thoughts. First we can go over the things that tend to overwhelm you.

Ruth: Okay.

Therapist: Ruth, when your cousin called you beaming about her new baby, your thoughts turned inward to your situation, rather than sharing in a wonderful experience of your cousin's. When this happens I call it riding the bus. In other words, when your attention is on your thoughts and feelings, you are metaphorically riding the bus. In our work together, one of the goals will be for you to take fewer bus rides. Moreover, you will need to notice when you are already on the bus in order to get off as soon as possible.

Ruth: Ha! I like that. In my case, I've been living on the bus—not just riding!

Therapist: Yeah. I can see you are suffering on the bus quite a lot. You have had a lot to deal with, and your brain seems to always need to chew on something. Your brain has been in overdrive with your psychological pain.

Ruth: How can I stop it? It's been impossible. I try to distract myself but nothing works.

Therapist: Ruth, it's important that you begin to look at your thoughts as outside of yourself. They are not you. With the metaphor of the bus, you need to look at them as external things coming into your mind—to your mental bus stop. All the while, you are the observer. You observe these feelings and thoughts. Some of them are good. Some of them are bad. Some of them are useful. Some of them are useless—or worse, harmful. But with all of them, you are just the observer.

Ruth: I see. But it's difficult to do.

Therapist: Yes, you are right. I know it must be frustrating and exhausting for you to experience so much emotion, but you can do it. When a thought or feeling arises, accept it, acknowledge it—you will not be able to help but feel it for a moment, but then do not go for the ride. View the thought and feeling as a bus with no destination. This will help you begin to separate yourself from your experience of the bus, which holds all the seats for your negative thoughts and emotions. You will then become the observer of the thoughts and feelings and this will allow you to separate from them.

Ruth: Okay. But then what?

Therapist: Then it is important for you to engage activities in which you find value—productive activities conducive to your happiness. This is similar to the work you did with focused breathing, concentrating on the feeling of the air molecules entering your nostrils, expanding your lungs, exiting your nostrils.

Ruth: It's so hard to concentrate on anything. I get so overwhelmed.

Therapist: Yes, I understand that your thoughts and feelings are overwhelming. As you work on this, you will develop the ability to engage in even the little things. In time, you will be focused on big things that reflect your core values and keep you off the bus.

Ruth: So explain how I can do this?

Therapist: Well, when you were talking to your cousin, you may have experienced a wave of emotion. Then you may have experienced a gut-wrenching empty feeling in your stomach. This is the bus arriving. When she spoke of her baby, you felt sadness and perhaps even envy. When you got off the phone, you began to dwell on your sadness about not being able to get pregnant. Your jealous feelings about your cousin result in bus riding. Is that about how it happened, Ruth? Is that what you experienced?

Ruth: Yes, right on target. That is exactly what I experienced and how I felt.

Therapist: The idea for you, Ruth, is to recognize the bus as external, not as yourself. Once you recognize it as a bus, do not get on. Instead, focus your brain on your plan. Your plan is for you and your husband to consult with a fertility specialist, subsequently following the medical instructions for a period of time. If this is not successful, reevaluate the situation and implement a new plan. Plans identify intended results—destinations in other words, while bus rides have no destination to begin with. The key here is to recognize the bus, then focus on the plan. If necessary, engage in focused breathing, and then fully engage in whatever your daily activity is at that moment. Remember, engaging one hundred percent is no easy task. It will take time to develop this ability. However, engaging one hundred percent brings about much healthier experience of life. When you are able to achieve such focus, you are off the bus.

Ruth: What if the thoughts and feelings come back?

Therapist: They will. When you notice them, view them as a bus. They are external. They are driving through or past you. They are not you. Engage fully in something, in a task, breathing, whatever is present.

Ruth: It is not easy to concentrate or engage in something when I am hit with such sad feelings.

Therapist: Yes, I understand. Sad feelings can be overwhelming. They can derail your plans if you let them. To get back on track, you must learn to persevere. Often, breathing will help you get off the bus, making it easier to focus intensely on what you are doing in the moment. I know it is difficult. Ruth, with this awareness and a lot of practice, you will become better and better at getting off the bus and enjoying your life in peace.

Ruth: Okay. I will try.

Therapist: That's what it's all about—trying. I know you will be able to turn this around.

Ruth continued in counseling where she was consistently supported and reminded by her therapist to get off the bus. She attended counseling on a monthly basis for a year. Ruth now experiences her life without the constant cloud of depression hanging over her. She is more productive at work and happier with her life at home.

Chapter 7

Living Life off the Bus

Having read this book, do you now observe your thoughts and sometimes your feelings as intruders, thieves of your life? Are you noticing how your peace of mind and satisfaction hinge upon your full engagement in whatever you are doing and that this intense present focus occurs without self-judgment and without thoughts of how or what others may judge?

Whether it is friends, family, exercise, recreation, education, contributing to your community or something else—have you gained an appreciation of the benefits of identifying and planning for what you value most?

Will you be more inclined to seek the support of your friends rather than withdraw and isolate? Are you now careful to spend only short times sharing bus ride stories with your friends and more time engaging in rewarding activities with those who care about you?

If you are stuck and suffering on the bus, are you now less resistant to seeking help from a therapist?

The bus metaphor and the other keys to emotional and behavioral health detailed in this book can make a significant positive difference in your life. They can be tools that can be applied to gain increased satisfaction and a richer, more meaningful life. Observing your thoughts, focusing on the present, and getting off the bus are a set of life-enhancing actions. The more you practice them, the more natural they will become. These actions can define whether you fully engage in your life or spend it in your head. This practice, one that could generally be called mindfulness, takes discipline. You are going to have to frequently remind yourself to let go of your thoughts and feelings, observe their passing, and refocus on life, just as it is, right in front of you, here and now.

Everyone with a mind suffers. The degree that you will suffer depends on your decisions. It is up to you to learn to get off the bus whenever you can. It is up to you to engage and focus in a mindful and meaningful life.

The goal of this book is to help you suffer less. This book provides you with the needed tools to achieve life satisfaction. Case studies of individuals who are trapped on the bus were illustrated to show you how they get off the bus and into living healthy lives. Exchanges between therapist and client exposed the healing process and how to get off the bus.

My hope is that after reading this book's therapist-client interactions the therapeutic alliance and the healing process will make sense. Because of this understanding you will become more comfortable with the idea of seeing a therapist. Consider seeing a therapist whenever you get stuck riding the bus and cannot get off of it on your own or with the help of your friends. Social support or a therapeutic alliance with a counselor is critical to getting off and staying off the bus as much as possible.

Becoming the observer of your thoughts and feelings can be enlightening. By looking more objectively at your thoughts and feelings you appreciate how these function to help you survive, solve problems and at times even prosper. You also realize how some thoughts and feelings make you suffer, especially if you find yourself repeatedly dwelling or obsessing on them. When the thoughts and feelings work against you and bring you suffering, it helps to look at these as intruders coming into and through you. This allows you a distance from them and enables you to engage more fully in life's possibilities.

Repetitive thinking and feeling patterns (riding the bus) are addictive. They catch you, stick to you, and they engage you in perverse, ineffective pseudo-problem-solving. Then they leave you exhausted with little to no forward progression. Applying the principles in this book will help you reduce suffering and improve satisfaction.

Becoming the observer and respecting the power of repetitive thoughts and feelings will be crucial in your quest to stay off the bus, reduce suffering, find peace, and gain a satisfying life.

Because the bus, repetitive thinking and feeling patterns, is insidious you will need an effective way of engaging in your life off the bus. To accomplish this goal you must know what you value in life and set a course of action that will enhance what you value. This is what we have termed a life plan. Having a life plan will provide you with a path that enables you to fully engage in and promote what you value. It will give you direction. Many of the cases presented show you how people lost focus on what they valued then, with the help of their therapist, they were able to get off the bus, engage in present focus and implement a life plan.

The metaphor of the bus prompts you to apply present focus to engage in actions that lead to your valued activities.

This book presents the keys to emotional and behavioral health in a simple and understandable way. However, you must recognize that in spite of the simplicity of the formula to get off the bus, riding the bus patterns are tenacious, addicting and ever-returning. Accordingly, staying off or getting off the bus is a lifelong journey.

Your view of the world may have changed as a result of the bus metaphor. Do you view your family members, boss, and coworkers differently when they complain, show you that they are in a bad mood or when they express wishes? Do you notice when they are riding the bus and letting their lives escape them?

Do you now notice how advertising puts you on the bus by creating a want or a fantasy that if you possessed that product you would somehow feel better about yourself? Do you project that others would view you with higher regard if you bought one of *those* cars?

Becoming mindful, present-focused and committed to live a life that reflects what you value is the quest. With this in mind, enrich your life and help others get off their buses. Stay focused and whenever possible let the bus go by as you choose your own way on your journey down life's path.

Neurofeedback

Neurofeedback is not a pill. It's training. It's a fitness program for the brain. But unlike going to the gym to build muscle, the brain holds onto its strengthening long-term. Over the past 20 years, thousands of children and adults who have received EEG neurofeedback have reduced or eliminated the need for medications and have improved functioning and performance. Without neurofeedback, many of these individuals would have continued to suffer from worry, stress, irritability and anger, mood swings, excessive cravings, insomnia, headaches, pain and poor concentration. EEG neurofeedback training has resulted in improved school performance, improved relationships, reduced pain, sustained sobriety and reduced psychological distress.

Neurofeedback training is endorsed by the American Psychological Association and the American Academy of Pediatrics for the treatment of problems related to concentration, impulsivity and hyperactivity. Neurofeedback is also used for anxiety and anger problems associated with autism.

Neurofeedback is a direct training of the brain. It trains the brain to know how to stay calm and focused and to avoid dysregulation (seizures, meltdowns, migraines, crying spells, panic attacks).

How is it done? Two or three forty-five minute training sessions are scheduled each week, for a total of twenty to thirty sessions. During the sessions, sensors are placed on the scalp with conducting paste and the brain waves are measured and sent to a computer. The computer screen displays a game or a movie. When your brain waves are in the "sweet spot" (calm and focused), the computer game advances or the movie gets bigger, brighter and louder. Repetition teaches your brain what it needs to do.

Call Dr. Steve at Comprehensive Psychological Services to discuss neurofeedback as a treatment option. He has been delivering neurofeedback services since 1996.

Phone: 801-483-1600

www.WeCanHelpOut.com

Comprehensive Psychological Services

Comprehensive Psychological Services (CPS) is a services mall for behavioral health professionals.

Licensed professionals, including prescribing physicians (MD & PA), psychologists (PhD & PsyD), Licensed Clinical Social Workers (LCSW), and Certified Mental Health Counselors (CMHC), who are located at Comprehensive Psychological Services enjoy the competence and tradition of excellence which CPS exemplifies.

Each of the professionals identified on our website are knowledgeable and effective independent practitioners. These professionals ascribe to evidence based treatment approaches and use outcomes feedback to derive positive results.

Our office support staff is highly trained and personable. Our facilities are modern, comfortable, and located on major public transportation routes.

We accept most health insurance plans. Call our office to see if the professional that you are interested in meeting is on your health plan or call to establish a fee without using your insurance.

Phone: 801-483-1600

www.WeCanHelpOut.com

The Autism Assessment and Treatment Center

Autism assessment and treatment for children and teenagers is our specialty. We recognize the importance of parent and teacher involvement in not only the evaluation but also the intervention process. We understand the impact that a youth with autism has on marriages, family relationships and siblings. Our services will lead to parent, teacher and child directed interventions that are designed to improve your child's or adolescent's functioning.

Our services begin with a comprehensive and multi-faceted evaluation. We identify your child's strengths and weaknesses. We administer the Autism Diagnostic Observation Schedule (ADOS), which is a state of the art evaluation instrument. Based on this evaluation we will recommend a treatment plan, which may include specialized therapies and trainings.

We customize our treatment to the identified needs and strengths of each child and family. We take a systemic philosophy in our approach, often working with family members as well as the individual. We deliver treatments that have been researched to be effective.

Please call us to learn more about our specialized services.

Phone: 801-386-8069

www.AutismUtah.com

Made in the USA
Monee, IL
21 January 2020

20635146R00079